Your First Job

For College Students—And Anyone Preparing to Enter Today's Tough Job Market

By
Ron Fry

Your First Job

For College Students—And Anyone Preparing to Enter Today's Tough Job Market

By
Ron Fry

CAREER PRESS
180 Fifth Avenue
P.O. Box 34
Hawthorne, NJ 07507
1-800-CAREER-1
201-427-0229 (outside U.S.)
FAX: 201-427-2037

YOUR FIRST JOB
FOR COLLEGE STUDENTS—AND ANYONE PREPARING TO ENTER TODAY'S TOUGH JOB MARKET
ISBN 1-56414-054-7, $9.95
Cover design by Harvey Kraft
Printing by Book-mart Press

To order this title by mail, please include price as noted above, $2.50 handling per order, and $1.00 for each book ordered. Send to: Career Press, Inc., 180 Fifth Ave., P.O. Box 34, Hawthorne, NJ 07507

Or call toll-free 1-800-CAREER-1 (Canada: 201-427-0229) to order using VISA or MasterCard, or for further information on books from Career Press.

Library of Congress Cataloging-in-Publication Data

Fry, Ronald W.
Your first job : for college students--and anyone preparing to enter today's tough job market / by Ron Fry.
p. cm.
Includes index.
ISBN 1-56414-054-7 : $9.95
1. Job hunting 2. College students--Employment. I. Title.
HF5382.7.F79 1993
650.14--do20 92-43446
CIP

Acknowledgments

I would like to thank all the people who tolerated me at *my* first job. They taught me by positive and negative example how to be a successful employee. It was, for me, a great learning experience that helped me, in part, gather the advice you will read in this book.

I am especially grateful to the people who helped me *before* I was employed for the first time. Like you, I am indebted to family members, teachers, friends, counselors, coaches and neighbors who assisted me in gathering the knowledge and experience that led to my first job.

I would also like to thank John Sherman for his insights on the topics covered in ***Your First Job***.

Now, turn to the Introduction on page 7. This, like the rest of your life, is an open-book test. Good luck.

Contents

Your First Job

Contents

Introduction

Are You Ready for Real World 101?

The Real World. You always knew you'd be facing it some day. "You won't say/wear/think/do that when you get out in the *real world*," your mother/teacher/father/obnoxious older sibling has been telling you for years.

Let me let you in on a secret: Don't be scared. Don't feel that, all of a sudden, you'd better get ready because you haven't been getting ready for, lo, these many years. Nope. You *have* been getting ready, you just may not have realized it.

That's one of the messages of this book, in fact. The purpose of ***Your First Job*** is to show you how to take all that stuff you already know, but may not *realize* you know, and turn it into a solid job-seeking and job-getting body of knowledge.

This book wasn't written to provide you with the tools to get a job. You already have the tools. I wrote this book to help you discover what great talents and experience you already have and how to use them to snag your first job.

10 easy steps

Let's look at what we're going to be talking about:

In Chapter One, we're reviewing where we're coming from so we know how to figure out where we're *going*. By the time you finish reading it, you'll be amazed at how much you've already learned and how well-prepared you really are for your first job.

Chapter Two helps you take your wonderful list of experience and education and put it on paper. It offers guidelines to producing just the right words on just the right kind (and color) of paper.

Just when you thought it was safe to leave the library...we come to Chapter Three. Researching the job will be one of the most important tasks in the whole pre-job process. I'll sum it up by saying, "It's who you know *and* it's what you know." And not necessarily in that order, either.

Now that you've got your resume and research ready, you begin the work of getting a job interview. Where are the jobs? What hidden meanings are to be found in the want ads? Do human resources personnel have hearts and souls? Chapter Four reveals all.

Your mom told you to shine your shoes, comb your hair and smile. And smile and smile and smile. Ah, the job interview. I'll help you discover that the process isn't slightly worse than being tortured by the Spanish Inquisition. Chapter Five will provide a lot of do's and don'ts for the interview.

Well, by golly, you had the interview and you got the job offer. What now? In this delicate interim period, there are even more recommendations on what to do and what not to do so that you land in the best position—and with the best salary—possible. That's what Chapter Six will do for you.

Chapter Seven assumes you took one of the jobs you were offered. It's the first of three chapters that reviews all the protocol surrounding the job itself. Is getting involved in office gossip really wise? How will your life be affected by the fact that you and your boss are both Type-A drivers? Is it a crime to make photocopies on the office machine of your party invitation? Will you be tested for drugs? Isn't life complicated? Chapter Seven will help sort all that out and give you advice for the rest of your career.

The next chapter still has you employed at the same place 90 days later. It will give you the groundwork for the first few months on the job. What I said in the last chapter still goes, but Chapter Eight takes you a bit beyond that and into the routine.

Chapter Nine gets even further into the intricacies of working, taking a close look at the annual review process and all the issues that entails. More hints, tips, no-no's and yes-yes's. A look at the lay of the land from your experience of 12 months on the job. And, we're already sniffing around at other jobs. We're not being fickle, we're being practical.

Then, finally, we come to Chapter Ten and we flat-out talk about it: Your *next* job. What will you do this time around that you did the first time? (Hint: A lot of the same.) How do you move to another job in the same department, the same company, a different industry? What if you're fired? What if you quit? What if you go to the cash register right now and buy this book?

Chapter One

Back to the Past

How You Began Preparing for Your First Job Years Ago

Mrs. Wiggles was right. It *did* matter what you did or did not do back in third-grade.

No, you don't have to accept the fact that putting a worm down the pants of the kid in front of you doomed you to a low-paying job forever. But, on a grander scale, what you did—and, sometimes more importantly, what you did *not* do—up to now can have an effect on getting and holding a job.

Let me explain: Without going into pages and pages of psychology, you and I both know that if you set yourself on fire in chemistry class, you probably were not destined for medical school. On the other hand, if putting a noun and verb together without causing anyone in the room to wince is beyond your capabilities, don't expect to be on the list for the Pulitzer Prize for journalism.

Career choices are made—or, at least, should in part be made—because you have an interest, an aptitude and a talent for certain subjects. You can force the issue sometimes, as you know from having studied very, very hard just to get a C in calculus. But you want to find a niche where you are comfortable and competent. (This is especially important if your job is performing brain surgery, but it is also important if you are doing my taxes or replacing my fan belt.)

When I say how do you do, I mean *how* do you do

Beyond choosing general job categories and then narrowing them down, you also have developed over the years an interest in and an inclination as to *how* you do things and a comfort level for such areas as public speaking, report preparation, etc.

A lot of this began many years ago. But elementary school is often where you and others discovered your talents, and where you also discovered that you did not like or simply couldn't get the grasp of other things.

It all boils down to this: What do you like to do? What are you good at doing? (What you like and what you're good at are probably the same things, but not necessarily.) If all goes well, your first (and all successive jobs) will allow you to be involved with what you enjoy and what you do well—while you avoid the disastrous stuff you hate and don't want to even think about. (If your response to the question, "Why don't you become a chemist?" is "I'd set the world on fire," it's important for all of us—you included—to know just what you mean by that.)

Let's look beyond the choice of careers. By this time in your life, you should be able to get within shooting distance of what you want to do, at least what kind of job you want to get *now*. So let's concentrate on how to sell yourself for a job that will satisfy you, allow you to show off your merits, help you avoid your demerits and give you a chance to land in a satisfying environment in which to learn and grow.

Learning doesn't stop with the day you finally finish school. You'd better hope you learn at your first job and at all other jobs or it will be a pretty boring life for you. The secret is finding the job that doesn't require so much learning you don't have a clue what's going on, but provides you the opportunity to do something that is challenging and fresh.

Back to the drawing board

You have been preparing for this first job all your life. If you were on a committee to decorate a bulletin board in third-grade, you learned something from that experience—group dynamics, art appreciation, visualizations, spatial relationships, meeting deadlines, pleasing the boss (the teacher) while pleasing the co-workers (the other kids), marketing the finished product, aesthetics, sharing the blame and the credit, and on and on.

All *that* from cutting out a few fish from green construction paper, you say? Definitely. And the more you worked with other people, the more you learned about them and about yourself. Do you, for example, want to get the work done right away so you can do something else? Or do you procrastinate until two hours before the deadline and do it all in a rush? Do you like working on a team or do you prefer working alone? Do you feel compelled to lead or do you want to fade into the woodwork (or the construction paper)?

There are a lot of questions you need to ask yourself, a lot of self-examining, to see what it is that you already know and what it is that you want from your career.

It's now time to list your strengths and what you want to get *strengthened* from this first job.

This exercise will lead us right into the next chapter, about writing resumes. After all, your resume should help you land a job that builds on what you're already good at and allows you to continue to perform tasks that you already do well.

If the personality profile fits, wear it

In another book I wrote for Career Press, ***Your First Resume***, I provided several pages of a "Where Do I Fit? Chart" so you could have a quick look at particular skills and some sample careers that depend on those qualifications. Check it out. It will give you a lot of material to work with when you build your list of strengths and weaknesses and likes and dislikes.

For example, one of the skills on that list is "negotiating." As shown on the chart, it's not just useful, it's *vital* in careers in politics, sales, psychiatry and social work. Do you rate yourself high, average or low in this area? Are you good at negotiating or do you avoid any form of it? Is it something you can do if you have to, but you don't seek it out?

Let's say you are good at negotiating. You've always been able to get opposing factions to work together, or to convince others to accept your ideas, even if the end result is a compromise on both sides. Does that mean that all of the above fields are open to you?

Hardly. Sales and psychiatry may come together only when the one sells the other one a couch. Be reasonable and identify aspects of your life that demonstrate where you have interests.

The point is this, however: If you think sales or politics is an area that holds a strong interest for you, but you avoid and even hate the thought of negotiating, then you'd better think again. Go back to the basics: What is it that you like to do and what do you already do well? And add this: What do you want to *learn* how to do?

Certain skills are necessary for virtually every job: Secretary of Labor Robert Reich says that "communication and critical skills that allow people to make judgments and solve problems" are far more important than the ability merely to show up on time and put in a productive day (although these habits and skills are vital, too). Computer skills are another must for the '90s. Knowledge of a foreign language opens horizons, literally, worldwide.

If you don't have the best training in one or more of these areas, it may limit the number of jobs you can apply for. At the least, you should determine to beef up your skills in these and other areas while working that first job through on-the-job training or after-hours classes.

"Marvin, you're 35 years old and you're gonna do what?!"

Before we go on to resume writing, think about this: Up until a couple of generations ago, it was unheard of for most people to switch careers once they were trained for something and began working in a particular field. Today, you probably know a lot of people who used to do one type of work and now do something entirely different. They may have even gone to—or returned to—college to become educated in a new field, perhaps one that did not even exist when they were getting their first job.

Your first job may also not be related to what you will be doing 20 years from now, or you might be in the same field, even at the same company. Whatever paths your career takes, this first job should be exciting and educational.

You first job may also teach you something extremely important: It may make you realize that what you thought you wanted to do for years and years is not what you want to do at all.

Remember that your "first job" began when you first began developing your work habits, your likes and dislikes, your skills, your interests in areas that have brought you to where you are now.

Think of your first job as part of a continuum. You will go on to other jobs and—the point of this chapter—you are now coming from a lifetime of training, education, experience and preferences that have formed and shaped *you*.

You're more prepared than you thought you were!

Chapter Two

Writing the Resume

The You, the Whole You and Nothing But You

The most important rule when writing your resume? Let's get right to it: Tell the truth. When you have finished writing your resume—as soon as you've read this chapter, no doubt—make sure it is *accurate* as well as complete.

Taking a rough edge and making it a rounded corner is one thing (we'll get to that in a moment). Telling flat-out fibs about yourself is something else again. If you do, you can expect one of the following to occur: 1) You'll get caught; 2) You'll feel guilty; or 3) Both.

You, too, can be proud of the truth

An important point to be made is that, moral issues aside, you don't have to lie. You've already created a *persona* that can be put on paper to impress the human resources people. Let's talk about how to do that.

Think of the preparation of your resume as an exercise in self-exploration. Who are you, *really*? How do you want to be perceived by others at your new job (when you get it, that is)? Think back to what I said at the beginning of the book—my comments on strengths and weaknesses, likes and dislikes, and so forth. Your resume should reflect who you are (all the experience and education that have formed you), yet you should focus your attention on the future—show how you have strengths that will make you a good employee in a particular position, company or industry. In a sense, a resume takes the reader back in time in order to move you *forward* in time.

Tell 'em what you're really like

A resume is a way to brag about yourself. The tone of the resume should reflect this. Tell the reader of the resume—probably someone who has never heard of you before and who is picking your resume out of a pile of other resumes on a desk—how solid, how accomplished you are and, very, very importantly, just how qualified you are for a specific position or, at the least, for a specific company.

Shine those shoes, metaphorically speaking

Appearances are vital. Just as you wouldn't go to a job interview looking a mess, your resume has to be on the "best-dressed list," too. Think of it this way: You aren't present to show off your snappiest interview clothes, your winning smile and your charming, concise answers to tough questions. You are sending your resume to represent you. (If everyone believed that, I wouldn't have recoiled in horror a few years ago when I got a job hunter's resume on shocking pink paper. It couldn't go in the trash can fast enough!)

Choose a dignified color. You can't go wrong with white. Light gray or off-white are good, too. And don't think that the more texture the paper has, the better. Less is more. Plain paper (a good 25 percent cotton bond, not photocopy paper) is better than a textured weave that cries out, "Notice me!"

With all the computers around these days, there's no excuse for not preparing your resume on a word-processing program and then printing it on a laser printer. If you don't own such equipment, someone you know and love does. Or, at least, someone does who will allow you to know and love them *for a slight fee*.

There's another big advantage to this computer-generated method: You can easily and quickly make changes in the resume to target various kinds of jobs (again, more on that later).

Not all resumes are created equal

In another Career Press book, ***The Smart Woman's Guide to Resumes and Job Hunting***, the authors have provided different versions—before and after—of the same person's resume. Each version is geared toward a specific position or job area. (If you're male, you'll still find this book an extremely useful resource tool.)

Don't, whatever you do, get cute with the type faces. Use something like Courier or Palatino, assuming you have options on your computer, and avoid the fancy and the flamboyant. You will want to print some of the headings in boldface, to make them stand out, and to give a strong overall appearance to the resume, but keep the amount of boldface on the page to a reasonable minimum. The same is true for words in all capital letters.

Without becoming compulsive-obsessive yourself, you'll probably want to keep printing out several versions—the same content, but with different type sizes, different headings in boldface, etc.—until you feel you've achieved just the right look. For a lot of good examples of various types of resumes, check out the many samples in my companion book, ***Your First Resume***.

Stand back!

Use this as a guide: The *content* of the resume gets you the interview, but its *appearance* will get it noticed. Before you submit a resume, place it on a table and really look at it. (Or do as I sometimes do—place it on the *floor* and stare down at it.) Is it as attractive as it possibly can be? Imagine your resume in a stack of 25 other resumes. How will it compete for the eye of the person selecting the top five candidates for interviews? Be your own harshest critic—don't pass that job on to someone in human resources at the Acme Sponge Company.

Check out these three computer programs that help you write your resume: ***Resume & Job Search Pro*** (Spinnaker Software Corporation); ***Easy Working Resume Creator*** (Spinnaker); and ***Individual ResumeMaker*** (Individual Software).

These programs give you tips on various aspects of resume-writing and even touch on other aspects of job hunting.

The nuts and bolts of it all

Put what I call "the data" at the top: Name, address and phone number. Personally, I prefer to spell out words like "street" and "avenue" because I think it looks better, although I readily use the post office's two-letter code for states. Yes, it's a very, very minor point and I agree that it is unlikely that anyone would refuse to hire you because you wrote down "123 Main St." instead of "123 Main Street," but a certain *savoir faire* about your resume is also important.

You can either stack the data (name on first line, street on second, etc.) or you can run them across the top of the page, with a line underneath. Try it different ways to see how it looks.

Where were you at precisely 4:27 p.m., June 16, 1991?

Earlier, I mentioned "rounding off the corners." What I really mean by this is, don't be totally literal or you'll jumble up your resume with too many numbers and dates. If you worked at, say, the Bijou Theatre from April 28, 1990, to December 15, 1992, are you going to tell everyone in the world the exact dates you started and stopped working? Does it really matter whether you began on April 28 or April 15 or April 3? Not really.

On your resume, write down "April 1990—December 1992" for the time spent on this job. A couple of jobs from now, in fact, you may want to drop the months and simply put "1990-1992." The further away you get from a job, the less specific you need to be about some of the information. And, in a few years, you will even drop some of the jobs, especially if they were part-time, or ones you held in college or in the summer only. (A friend of mine once worked four—count 'em—four hours at a department store before realizing he was meant for greater things. You can be sure his lightning-fast retail career doesn't appear on his resume!)

If you have very little job experience, you can still produce a resume that *sells*. First, it has to look good (I won't stop saying that, will I?). Second, it has to summarize the *qualities* you have: the experience and the education that qualifies you for this job.

Let's look at how one college senior prepared his resume (see next page) for his first job:

AARON BENJAMIN
4175 Central Avenue
Brambleton, IL 60999
(312) 555-6775

Job Objective:	Writer in Corporate Publications Department
Education:	Bachelor of Arts, Indiana University, 1993 Major: Journalism/Minor: Government GPA: 3.5/4.0
Related: Experience:	*Indiana Daily Student* (Student Newspaper): Features Editor, 1992-93 Editorial-Page Editor, 1991-92 Staff Reporter, 1990-91
Work Experience:	*Brambleton Weekly Times*: Reporter, Business Department, Summers, 1990-1992 Wrote features on business owners and other business-related news in Brambleton area; edited copy of other writers. Trained new interns in business department.
Honors/Awards:	Ernie Pyle Scholarship, Journalism Department, 1990 Finalist, Sigma Delta Chi writing awards, 1991
Community Activities:	Member, Steering Committee, Cancer Awareness Campaign Responsible for disseminating information (writing ad copy, public speaking) on health issues to campus audiences Vice President, Big Brothers Campus Chapter Founded and developed first membership drive for college Big Brother program; increased chapter membership by 150% in 3 months.

Any line-item kudos here?

Let's look at these items, one by one:

Job Objective.

Aaron is applying for a specific opening. A company is seeking a writer for its publications staff. (You will notice that he even brings up his writing experience in his volunteer work.) With his handy computer, he can change this job objective to read "Features Writer on Daily Metropolitan Newspaper" or "Write and Edit Publications for Nonprofit Association" and on and on.

Education.

Not much you can change here. His GPA is noteworthy enough to bring to the attention of the reader of this resume. If yours isn't something you have ever written home about (other than to say, "Mom, I'm doing the best I can!!"), leave this item out. A "2.0/4.0" notation won't win interviews even though you may end up being a better employee than someone with a higher GPA.

Related Experience.

Don't go too far back into your past. Editing the girl scout newsletter in sixth-grade is a bit much, but recent activities are worth noting. Aaron has identified the newspaper for the reader who may not have heard of it. His positions on the paper are in chronologically descending order and are kept short and sweet. If anything extraordinary happened, of course, Aaron would have mentioned it. Don't wait for the interview to say, "Oh, and by the way, I did get two Pulitzers while I was the features editor."

The "related experience" may well change depending on the "job objective," although Aaron seems bent on a career in the writing field. Small changes can be important, however, and lift you out of that proverbial pile of resumes on the desk. Suppose, for example, that Aaron was seeking a position with a nonprofit organization devoted to a particular cause and it just happened that he wrote a series of articles on that cause for the campus newspaper. "Wrote six-part series on women's health issues" may be just enough to get the reader to pick up the phone and tell him to come on down...with writing samples.

Work Experience.

Again, you'll emphasize what you think this reader will want to see. Here, Aaron is promoting his work in the business area since he is seeking a job in a corporation. However, he may also have worked several hours a week on the sports desk—if it's a sports job he's after, then, of course, he'll promote the heck out of that side of the work he did for the weekly.

Honors/Awards.

Don't go too far back for this one, either. A writing award in high school won't mean anything for the reader and it may even cause a bit of nose-wrinkling. Aaron hasn't given any details of those he is mentioning. If the interviewer wants to find out why, he or she will ask—or Aaron can plan to bring them up at the interview. The exception is, once again, if the honors or awards are relevant to this particular job slot. If that six-part series got Aaron the eye of Sigma Delta Chi, it will also impress the interviewer at the Women's Health Center.

Community Activities.

Surely you've done *something* besides study, sleep and party? A little notation, as Aaron has done, is a good idea to give the reader a clearer view of what you did and what the organization or cause is all about. Now, Aaron may have spent only part of one semester with Big Brothers, but that's OK. What is important is that he was conscientious enough to get involved in something and he took an active role, and wasn't just a passive member who paid his dues and never attended a meeting. And, as I mentioned earlier, he has even tied it in with his job objective.

References.

It's not necessary to indicate on your resume that references are available. But have names, addresses and phone numbers ready; provide references only after you've asked permission to do so from the references. Never, never give out names without consent. It's simply good manners. It also gives people time to refresh their memories. Other than a bad reference, there's not much worse than a vague one. ("Was he in scouts? Are you sure? I can't remember him. Did he save that kid's life? No, that was his brother. Now, his brother, *he* was the smart one!")

Note, also, that Aaron has quantified one of his activities ("150% in 3 months"). If you've helped an organization or an employer achieve something, put it down.

Don't ruin your resume's health

Let's consider what Aaron didn't include in his resume—no photo, no personal information, no salary requirements, no mention of affiliations with controversial political groups or causes. This is wise. Aaron's resume focuses on the skills and experiences that are pertinent to the job—no more.

I cringe whenever I see a resume that tells me the applicant's martial status, height and weight, age and health condition. This is unimportant, irrelevant and inappropriate for a resume. It can also be dangerous to your chances of landing an interview.

Stick to the items on Aaron's resume, possibly adding a "Skills" category if, for example, you have significant computer experience or you're fluent in a foreign language.

For lots and lots of other examples of resumes, check out the two books mentioned in this chapter, ***Your First Resume*** and ***The Smart Woman's Guide to Resumes and Job Hunting***.

Get your coat. We're going to the library.

Chapter Three

Job Research

Finding Out What You Need to Know In Order to Land the Job

And you thought that once you finished your last term paper, your research days were over. Think again, Sherlock.

I'm not comparing you to the famous Mr. Holmes for nothing. While you may never have occasion to say to your prospective CEO, "I see by the red dirt on your boots that your company has an iron mine in Bolivia," you do need to know, before your interview, whether the company *does* have an iron mine in Bolivia.

In your quest to track down clues about your prospective employer, the library is your best friend. While it isn't the only source of information to be discussed in this chapter, it is the central one.

You are visiting the library to find out as much information as you can on: 1) a whole industry; 2) a particular company; and 3) individuals connected with that company.

The industry itself, being the most general topic of the three, will probably be the subject of several books and have its own trade magazines. (A trade magazine is a publication that deals exclusively with one industry and is read by members of that industry. For example, *Editor & Publisher* is written for people working on newspapers.)

If you are looking for a job in your college major, you should already be somewhat familiar with the industry. (If you aren't, you slept through more seminars than you should have.) But you may not have thought of "the industry" and you in the same breath until now.

Through reference books and computerized information sources (InfoTrac, ABI Inform and others) you can find newspaper articles, magazine articles, trade magazines, books and other sources on the industry—and possibly on individual companies as well.

Tell the reference librarians what you are doing and they'll help you find even more sources. And, if they don't have it, they can often request it on an inter-library loan from another library elsewhere in your state.

Once you get to the level of reading about a particular company and the individuals associated with it, newspaper clippings in the library's vertical files, local and regional magazines and newspapers, business journals and so forth will be helpful. Here are a few helpful directories you'll find in the reference section of the library:

- ***Moody's Industry Review***
- ***The Career Guide: Dun's Employment Opportunities Directory***
- ***Ward's Business Directory of U.S. Private and Public Companies***
- ***Dictionary of Occupational Titles (Bureau of Labor Statistics)***
- ***Occupational Outlook Handbook (Bureau of Labor Statistics)***

- ***Dun & Bradstreet Million Dollar Directory***
- ***Standard and Poor's Register of Corporations, Directors, and Executives***

Good equation: Network > Net worth

I'd devote a few, hard-working hours in the library first, then I'd start networking. If you talk to people before you've done any groundwork, you'll not know as many questions to ask and you'll be wasting your time and theirs. Go to them armed with information—lots of semi-educated questions and then, based on their answers, return to the library to look up more information.

With whom do you network? Professors teaching courses in the area you're interested in; professionals working in the area; people currently and formerly working for the companies you have in mind; the authors of or the subjects of articles in newspapers and magazines; reporters and editors on business journals who write about the company and the industry; friends who have the same academic major.

I'm not here for a job interview—honest!

Make appointments for "informational interviews" with people who are likely to be able to advise you on how to get a job in the industry or with a particular company. Ask for 30-45 minutes of their time and tell them you will be seeking their advice. They will be flattered, a key reason they will probably give you the time.

If they don't know you, share your background and your interests with them briefly, and then ask them to recommend places to apply, methods to use and other people to contact (both for information and for job interviews). Ask for their views on the future of the industry (will job openings increase in the next 10 years or is the business going down the tubes?), which places are "good places to work" (is it the sort of place where the slogan "Beatings will continue until morale improves" is a joke or for real?), and on and on.

If you are on time, dressed well, prepared with questions, alert and polite, you have gotten off on the right foot during this very important process. If you leave a good impression, this person may well allow you to use his or her name in contacting someone for a job interview. Leaving your resume with your contact is a good idea. He or she may hear of a job opening a month later and be kind enough to give you a call—"It sounds like your background is what they're looking for over at the bank. Tell Freddie (Mr. Frederick X. Smuggs to you) I said to call."

Send your "information interview" person a thank-you note. Promptly. It shows you have good manners and it reminds the person, in the midst of other work, that you were the Bright Young Thing who graced the office doorway three days before.

And, hey, who knows? You honestly went to see this guy on an informational interview but he ended up being so impressed with you that he offered you a job. I'll say it again: It could happen. (This brings up a point: Conduct yourself during the informational interview in the same way you will during a "real" interview. If you are late, don't dress well, and/or otherwise make a negative impression, is this person *really* going to recommend you to someone else? Memorize the rules in Chapter 5 before you ever show up for an informational interview.)

And, if you never use them, they'll look good on the coffee table

When you have identified companies that interest you, call their marketing departments and ask for literature on their products or services. This information, if available, may provide a lot of good background material for your interview. If you walk into an interview with absolutely no knowledge of the company and the interviewer says to you, "Well, what do you know about us?" and you hem and haw and stare at the scuff mark on your shoes, you might as well have stayed home. On the other hand, if you say things like, "My neighbor says that your CEO is a manic-depressive," you probably won't get the job either. Somewhere in the middle of these two responses is one where you share brief information on the company to show that you did at least *some* research.

Get ready to stop reading

If you know anyone working for a particular company you want to work for, put this book down and call them.

They can be your most valuable source of information—with a little grain of salt. If one contact happens to be a complainer and whiner, you'll get such a negative view that you'll cross the company off your list forever. She may well be telling you the truth about "sweatshop" conditions, but she may also be working in a completely different area of the firm under a person who would never be the boss of the area you're looking at. And she may just be the sort of person who, when shown a glorious rainbow at the end of a storm, says, "There's not enough blue."

Be suspicious of the too-glowing report, on the other hand. The person you're talking to may be afraid you'll reveal him as the source of negative information to his boss. Or he may simply be an anti-whiner and make everything sound perfect. That's why it's good to talk to as many people as you can from different parts of the company. Merging their comments together will help you get a reasonably clear picture of what to expect. If the comment, "Acme Sponge really treats its employees fairly," keeps coming up in these conversations, it's a pretty safe bet that it has a good working environment.

If you can get specific information on a job opening, on the supervisor of that job, on your potential fellow employees, etc., you've passed second base and the ball is still flying to center field.

You may not be able to push your questioning too far if the person you are talking to is someone now working in the department with the job opening. She doesn't want to be perceived as a "tattle-tale," nor does she want to tell you glowing stuff and then, once you're hired, confess that it really isn't all that great and she's doing the Great & Rapid Job Hunt Shuffle to get out of there herself.

Keep your questions to specific tasks ("How many reports like that do you do in a month's time?") and you'll probably learn far more. If she lets it be known that the reports are always late, that the boss never accepts the report the first time, that continual editing and rewriting goes on, that other departments complain about missing deadlines...well, you decide if that's the environment you want to jump into.

It's fair to ask, "What sort of person is Jane Smith to work for?" and let the other person decide what they're going to say. Frankly, how good and how close a friend you are to this person will help determine what she tells you. If you're old friends, she'll be frank and help you balance the negative with the positive. If you have been brought together by a mutual friend and this is your first meeting, you'll learn the more general stuff. Questions about turnover (asking how long she's worked there and how long the person worked there who is now being replaced) will give you some idea as to the stability—and working environment.

The mutual friend may end up almost being a better source. If he tells you that the employee he put you in touch with constantly complains about the unfair treatment from the supervisor (dear Jane Smith, who may soon be *your* supervisor), maybe you should keep looking elsewhere.

Asking about salary

How do you know how much you might be paid? Some ads for jobs will tell you a salary figure (or a salary range), but most do not. Bring this up in your informational interviews. The person you are asking isn't under any pressure to provide an exact, correct amount, yet he or she can probably come pretty close. Make sure you couch the question in terms of *your* experience and education, not in more general terms: "Mr. Henderson, with my education and experience, what do you think I could expect to make in that job over at Acme Sponge?"

Don't take Mr. Henderson's word as gospel. Ask as many people as possible and look at the different figures. They'll all probably be fairly close to one another. Armed with this information, you're in a position to decide if you want to pursue the job for that kind of money in the first place, and, if you do, to know whether this will be the approximate amount you will be offered. (We'll get back to the all-important questions about salary in the upcoming chapters.)

Again, the library will be helpful. Sources there, such as ***The American Almanac of Jobs and Salaries*** and ***The Occupational Outlook Handbook***, will show you average salaries for certain kinds of jobs, broken down by regions of the country and other sub-categories. Also survey the "Help Wanted" ads for jobs similar to the ones in question.

Remember, too, that some jobs will be paid on commission, and some employees will be rewarded (and have more job security) if they work in the revenue-producing areas of the company.

Your network: Don't let it fade away

One last recommendation: Don't forget what you learned in networking for your first job. Networking never dies. Keep in touch with the people who were helpful to you—all those people you interviewed in person or on the phone. Remember how you found out information in the library. Begin reading, if you haven't already done so, the trade publications you have unearthed. Allow yourself to become a part of other people's networks—you may soon be on the other side of the desk for an "informational interview." When it is time to move on to another job, another company, or even an entirely different career, you will have your custom-made network in place.

Chapter Four

How to Land a Job Interview

Putting Your Foot in the Door and Not in Your Mouth

Your crisp, perfect resume has been printed multiple times in a handful of versions. You have paid your dues spending hours reading and listening, seeking to discover all that you can about the industry you wish to work for, the company or companies you are interested in and the people involved in those companies. It's now time to find where the jobs are—and go for it. Here are some ways to go after the jobs—and land the interviews:

1. Respond to newspaper ads

A lot of people firmly believe in two things: The sun always rises in the east and you never get a job through the ads in the newspaper. They're right all the time about the sun (so far). They're right a lot of the time—but not all the time—about the want ads.

Why are some people prejudiced against the classified ads we have all read in the Sunday newspaper? There are several reasons. One, many people get jobs because of who they know (remember our discussion of networking?). Two, a lot of jobs are never advertised. Three, tons of jobs are filled from within a company. Even so, newspaper ads account for a great number of job placements. So why eliminate *any* job opportunities by ignoring the classifieds? My advice is pursue all job avenues—including newspaper want ads—and increase your odds.

If you're lucky, the newspaper has the jobs divided into categories ("Medical" or "Sales") so you can concentrate on certain areas and not have to read every ad, page after page.

After you've read enough ads, you will be a better judge of whether something is for you. Do be realistic. If they ask for three years of experience and you have three months, skip it and go on. On the other hand, if you are *close* to what they are looking for—you're short only a few months, for example—then go for it, especially if you think your work experience or background will make up for the shortfall.

Blind ads: A caveat before pursuing

"Blind" ads aren't all bad ("A computer-software company in the Paramus area is..."), but you are at a much greater advantage if you know which company you're actually applying to. Also, keep in mind that many companies use blind ads just to scout the available talent and salary expectations. There may not actually be a job opening so don't be surprised if you never get a call after responding to such an ad.

And finally, you should be aware of the *biggest* risk when following up on a blind ad: If you are currently employed, you just might be contacting your own company! To avoid this embarrassing—and potentially dangerous—situation, request that your response not be forwarded to your current employer when submitting your resume to the box number.

Other situations to look out for when responding to newspaper ads—blind or otherwise: Certain words can be used loosely. "Marketing" and "telemarketing" are perfectly legitimate words, but they are often used to describe semi-legal operations where people wearing telephone headsets, crowded in a "boiler room," seek to sell products over the phone to people who can't afford them.

Words like "sales" or "representative" can also be stretched to imaginative lengths.

If the promised salary looks too good to be true, thank P.T. Barnum for his eloquent "There's a sucker born every minute." And I have a friend who never answers ads that have more than one exclamation mark. (Choose your own prejudices.)

Responding to the ad: Cover letters are key

Write a short, to-the-point cover letter to accompany your resume when responding to an ad. See the example on the next page.

Marie has provided the details of the ad itself. This company may have placed 20 ads in 50 different newspapers last week. She helps them. She did not, however, go into many details. After all, her resume is enclosed and it should speak for itself. But she does highlight the fact that she is qualified, that she is eager to work for this company and that she knows simple rules of politeness.

This letter, like the resume, is on the computer. All Marie has to do is change a few words and phrases and it's a whole new letter.

And once the letter has been sent? If you didn't know anything about this company beforehand, do the basic

Sherman Johnson
Director, Human Resources
Smutch and Company
123 Main Street
Deerfield, MN 22222

Dear Mr. Johnson:

I am replying to your advertisement for a "Sales Representative" in the Sunday, November 3, edition of The Duluth Bugle. Enclosed is my resume.

The description of the Sales Representative for Smutch and Company matches the kind of position I am seeking.

As noted on my resume, I have considerable sales experience. I would appreciate the opportunity to put that experience to work for you.

Thank you for your consideration. I look forward to hearing from you.

Sincerely yours,

Marie Judson

Marie Judson

enclosure

research we discussed earlier. Make a few calls to people who may know someone who works there or who knows about the corporate culture (the all-important phrase that we'll discuss later in this book).

It is always helpful if one of your networking contacts offers to call someone he or she knows at the company you're contacting. In Marie's case, for example it could have worked like this: Ed Jones on her networking list calls Martha Smith in the marketing department at Smutch & Co. She, in turn, makes a call to human resources and says something like this:

> "A good friend of mine whose judgment I respect has called to recommend Marie Judson for that sales rep position that Jerry advertised for. She sent in her resume earlier this week."

That kind of contact will pull Marie's resume out of the pile. Then, it's up to her (and her education, experience and overall impression created by her resume) to take over. But, the important thing is, she's been singled out. The chances of her being interviewed have shot upward.

If, through your research after you mailed the letter, you discover that you've applied to a company that people are fleeing like flies, you may have wasted the postage, but you've saved yourself a big headache. If they call for an interview, you can always say, "I'm sorry, but I'm no longer available." You need not complete the sentence with the phrase "because informed sources tell me that everyone in management at your company is psychotic."

Fortunately, this kind of situation is the exception to the rule. You can't research everything as thoroughly as you'd like, nor do you want to wait until you can get to the library when the ad is in today's paper and you want to get the letter/resume in the mail tonight. If it looks and sounds legitimate and appropriate for you, go ahead.

2. Contact companies you want to work for, even if there are no openings

Let's say that Mugwump Enterprises is a place you have always wanted to work for, or it's someplace you kept reading good things about during your job-hunt research. If you know of nothing that's available right now, don't let that stop you. Get over there and fill out an application.

Better yet, take a blank one with you ("I'll fill this out and mail it to you right away") and have it photocopied several times. Fill out the photocopied ones as many times as you need to until you are satisfied you have just the right answers typed into just the right spaces, transfer the information to the good copy and mail it back with a nice cover letter. Stress the areas where you are interested in working (Customer Service, Publications), but make it plain that you will be pleased to come in to talk with someone about "various job openings at Mugwump." Don't gush, but indicate that you respect the company and say it's one you'd like to work for.

When you are at Mugwump, of course, ask in the human resources office to see a list of current job openings. If any of them do sound interesting, direct your application toward them.

Send in a resume with the application. You've worked hard on it, it looks good and it is how you want to be represented. Even though 80 percent of the information is also on the application, there may be an important 20 percent that is not. Suppose that you show on your resume (but not on your application) that you have volunteered for years with Big Brothers/Big Sisters and just suppose that the person reading the application thinks that's the best cause around—move to the top of the stack, brother/sister!

Visiting the company can also give you a brief but sometimes important view of the place. Not only do you see a bit of the physical plant, you also get to observe real, live employees in singles, pairs and bunches. How do they dress—corporate or casual? Are they smiling? Is it noisy? Clean? If you're allowed, go to the employee cafeteria to get a soft drink or a cup of coffee. More snooping.

Employee newsletters can also provide you with some, albeit edited, information on the company. How are employees treated? Does the newsletter lavish praise (and photo coverage) on the CEO or do employees in management and support areas receive a fair share of the praise (and photos). Ask for any other materials about the company. There might be a corporate brochure that will give you more of a glimpse at life inside.

3. Let everyone know that you are looking for a job

In your job research, you let a lot of people know that you were preparing to enter the job market. Now it's time to let your networking contacts know that you *are* entering the market—with a vengeance. Ask them for leads. Do they know of any openings? Would they please keep you in mind if they hear of anything? Do they know anyone over at Mugwump? And on and on.

Send your contacts a copy of your resume, with a cover note, asking them to review it "at their convenience" (a polite phrase) and to let you know if they have any recommendations where you might send it.

Be sure to let them know where you have already applied or plan to apply—that alone can jog their memories, causing them to say, "Hey, I know the VP of Sales over there. Let me give him a call." And, just to make sure they do touch base with the VP, immediately send them brief thank-you notes, expressing appreciation for their offer to contact that person on your behalf. If they forgot, this will remind them.

Always be polite. Always be prompt. Always send thank-you notes—short ones without exclamation marks. These habits alone can get you work. ("That nice young man from Central State always sends me a thank-you note after we've talked. Harry, don't you have a vice presidency open over at Mugwump?")

4. Use your placement office

Don't forget, in all the hubbub of getting ready to go to work that, if you are a college student, you should have, nearby, a great source of information on job openings: Your placement office.

And, depending on the college, this should be available to recent graduates as well as current students. You may be able to contact the placement office through an on-campus computer system or you may need to go there in person.

Whether the information is on a disk or on paper, it should give you some good leads. And, a distinct advantage is that the jobs should all pretty much fall into your category of experience and education. After all, why would a company send a notice of an opening at the vice president's level to a college placement office?

Job fairs and recruitment drives by companies on campus are, of course, other ways to seek employment. Take with you plenty of copies of your resume and gather as much company literature as possible.

5. Check into employment agencies

You may be familiar with a number of names—executive recruiters, search firms, personnel agencies, headhunters—to describe businesses that assist others in finding jobs, or help businesses find qualified employees. Be aware that not all of them work the same way. For example, executive recruiters, also known as headhunters, work for companies seeking high-level experienced candidates. Their client is the company rather than the individual. It's not likely that an executive recruiter would be incredibly helpful to you, a new entrant in the job market.

You may want to approach an employment agency to assist you in finding a job. Also referred to as placement firms, employment agencies take on both job seekers and companies as clients, and frequently place employees at entry-level positions.

Be careful, however, that you understand how the agency works. Although it's generally the employer who pays the agency upon placement of an individual, sometimes the job candidate is required to pay the fee. Be sure you have a clear understanding of how things work before you sign any agreement.

The biggest drawback to working with an employment agency is that you might be tempted to put too much faith in the agency, and bow out of an active job search. Again, working with as many sources—including employment agencies—as possible only maximizes your chances to land a job. Take advantage of the services of an employment agency, but continue pursuing all other job avenues available to you.

How to make sure your resume doesn't get buried in HR

"Human Resources" sounds like the place where they find people. Well, it is. Some companies still call it "Personnel" and others have named it "HR." Whatever. Depending on the company, the human resources office can be the place resumes go to die. But it doesn't have to be that way.

First of all, call the company and find out the name and exact title of the person in charge of the area you're interested in. Get the direct phone number of the person, if you can. (It's a lot more convenient than going through the busy main number every time.) Confirm the spelling of the person's name with his/her secretary. (Switchboard operators, I have found, can be deadly wrong when they try to spell someone's name, especially if it *sounds* like a common name. Trust the secretary instead. "Mr. Jon Browne" may be tired of seeing his name spelled "Mr. John Brown.")

Send that person a resume and a short cover letter. If you have permission from anyone, include a name in the letter. ("An acquaintance of mine, Tom Rogers of the mayor's office, suggested I contact you." Don't exaggerate. If Tom's merely an acquaintance, say so. Don't turn him into a friend. Imagine the letter being read over the phone to Mr. Rogers. That should keep you honest.)

In the cover letter, explain that you'll follow up with a phone call "in a few days' time" and that you'd appreciate the opportunity to meet with him to discuss employment opportunities there.

Make a note in your calendar—name and phone number—for four or five *business days* later. Take holidays and weekends into account. Give the letter a chance to arrive, to be read by the secretary and to be read by the individual. It's hard to imagine, but your letter and resume will not be the most important piece of mail to cross that person's desk.

Call on the day you've marked on the calendar. A good secretary will remember the letter. He or she will probably tell you one of several things: 1) The letter was forwarded to human resources; 2) Mr. Browne hasn't seen it yet; 3) he has seen it and the secretary doesn't know if he wants to talk with you yet; 4) he wants to make an appointment; or 5) he will "no doubt" call you.

A watched phone never rings

Then you play the Eternal Waiting Game. To keep it from driving you crazy, have a dozen Mr. Brownes in the fire. To keep from saying embarrassing things to someone on the other end of the line (you discover four sentences into the phone conversation that the Mr. Browne you are speaking to is Mr. Bob Brown of Allied Computers and not Mr. Jon Browne of The Sheldon Companies), keep a "cheat sheet" taped up next to the phone. Have the names, titles and company names of all persons you have contacted. When Mr. Browne calls, he'll probably say, "Hi, this is Jon Browne!"—and you have to think *fast*.

The secretaries and administrative assistants of this world hold tremendous power. They can make or break you and they know it. Be polite, but never patronizing, and, very importantly, keep your calls brief and to the point. No small talk, other than a friendly mention of the blizzard going on outside your windows, and on to the topic at hand.

You don't butter her bread

Remember, the secretary owes his or her loyalty to the boss, not to you. You may never know whether the boss has ever seen your resume. The secretary may have forwarded it to human resources (it could be strict company policy) or the boss may, as we speak, be reading it with great excitement.

Don't push too hard. Don't call several times a week or continue to send letters. In fact, don't send even a second letter if you don't hear the first time. If Mr. Browne turns out to be of no help (you can't get past his secretary's "He's in a meeting and won't come out until the Balkans are at peace"), go ahead and send another resume and cover letter to the human resources office.

Follow-up activities

If Mr. Browne does send you a note saying he hasn't anything at the moment, but he has forwarded your resume to human resources, send him a short thank-you note (use your letterhead for these thank-you's, not a thank-you note card). If he turned out to be a very courteous, interested person who just didn't have any openings in his department, keep him in your files for future jobs. If you've suitably impressed him, he may remember you down the road.

Speaking of human resources offices: Check in periodically to see if there are additional openings. Find out the system at a company for posting new openings for "external hires." Some jobs, as we've mentioned, will be open only to those people who already work for the company. Naturally, that's preferred in many instances, as the company doesn't have to pay all the money to hire someone brand-new, train them and then hope they work out.

But, of course, there are jobs that are available to anyone—inside or outside—who qualifies. Does the company release these positions (complete with printed job descriptions, minimum qualifications and maybe even salary ranges) every Monday? Every other week? Find out, write it down and then swing by the human resources office on the day the new jobs are publicized.

The big silent treatment: Don't take it personally

Many human resources offices have a policy of not talking with you unless they are actually interviewing you, but it's worth a try to get a pre-interview at a company you especially want to work for. Call and ask for the person in charge of hiring in your area. Say you are interested in working for the company, that you have a resume and/or application on file at the company (be prepared to give the date you submitted it) and ask if you might come in to discuss "job opportunities."

Even if the person says no, if you have held up your end of a good, business-like phone conversation, she might be intrigued enough to pull your file, especially when you work into the conversation some information about yourself that sounds like you would fit in well with the company. ("I have a strong interest in using my copywriting skills in print advertising—I'm very impressed with your current campaign to market your new line of laser printers.") The human resources person may not even know there are ads out there for a "new line," but she will no doubt be impressed and may even note your comments in the corner of your application. Hey, it's worth a shot.

Should you get wild and crazy? You've probably read about someone who sent a resume by carrier pigeon or who paid a skywriter to fly his name and phone number over the company he wanted to work for. My recommendation is: Spend your time at the library, at the computer cranking out more resumes or on the phone checking with your networking contacts for new job leads. The only exception would be if the job you are after calls for an enormous amount of creativity (you're up for a job as the designer of skywriting messages for Wild and Crazy Billy's Enterprises), then you might go for the "wild and crazy" route. Otherwise, people will smile as they pull your resume out of the pile and carefully toss it in the trash can. Nobody likes a show off.

Keeping track of your job hunt activity

As you can guess by now, you have to be a super recordkeeper or all of this will fall apart at the seams and you'll end up *not* applying to your favorite company, or applying six times—and having all six applications trashed.

Use the computer, if you have one, or at least a typewriter, especially if your handwriting is illegible even to you, to keep track of each application. However you do it, keep a record of each company you apply to—the best way is to track it by company name and by the name of the person you've contacted. Then, when Mrs. Moore of Haan Condominiums calls, you can quickly find the information by searching under "Moore" or "Haan Condos."

Keep this information either on the computer screen or on big cards or full sheets of paper, filed alphabetically. Keep a running commentary to yourself on the status of each one. For example:

HAAN CONDOMINIUMS
3885 West 22nd St., P.O. Box 8887
Oklahoma City, OK 44432-8887
(405) 555-1239 Main Number
555-1223 Barbara Rush (Thelma Moore)
555-1228 Bill Macintosh
555-3399 Human Resources

3/1 Telephone—Mrs. Thelma Moore, secy to Barbara Rush, Dir. of Publications (rec. by Bob Land, First Nat'l. Bank) TM said to get app from HR/Send her a copy

3/5 Appl. at HR

3/7 Mailed app/res to HR / copy to TM with cover letter

3/14 Called TM—3x

3/15 Called TM—rec'd, BR reviewing.

3/22 TM called—appt. with BR's asst. dir., Bill Macintosh, 3/29 4:30 p.m., "possible opening for entry-level writer," samples of writing

3/29 Interview—left photocopies samples

3/31 TY to BM

4/15 TM called—second interview with BR, 4/22 3:00 p.m.

4/22 Interview with BR

4/23 TY to BR

4/30 Human resources (Jane Gardner) called—job offer! "Staff Writer, Publications Department"—report to BM—Second appt. with BM on 5/12 3 p.m. to discuss.

Let's review. First of all, keep the complete mailing address, company name and telephone number(s) at the top of your record. You won't realize how many times you'll need this until you *don't* keep it in a handy place.

Qk & drty rkd

This is a quick and dirty record of what has happened with Haan Condominiums. Just as you have done in class for years, create your own abbreviations (just remember to be consistent so that you'll remember what they mean).

Write down the date of the action and brief notes about what happened. In this example, you called the director of publications, based on the recommendation of a guy you know at the bank. You spoke to the director's secretary (and told her about Bob Land's recommendation). She said for you to get a job application in human resources, send them a copy and send her a copy.

You picked up the application on March 5 and mailed it two days later to both human resources and Mrs. Moore.

A week later, you tried to reach Mrs. Moore three times and her phone was busy each time. (This is called "reality.")

The next day, you reached Mrs. Moore who told you that her boss was "reviewing" your application.

A week later, she called you to say that there was a possible opening for an entry-level writer; she made an appointment with you to meet with her boss' assistant, Bill Macintosh. She told you to bring samples of your writing.

Before the interview, you made photocopies of the samples so you could leave them with Mr. Macintosh.

You sent Bill a thank-you note two days after the interview.

Mrs. Moore called two weeks later and made an appointment for you to meet with her boss.

A day after the interview, you sent Mrs. Rush a thank-you note.

A week later, Jane Gardner of the company's human resources department called to say that the company was pleased to offer you a position as a staff writer, reporting to Bill Macintosh.

She makes an appointment with you to meet with Bill in two weeks to discuss the job offer.

Nobody promised you a rose garden...this year

One important note that you've probably already picked up on: You called Haan Condominiums on March 1. The job offer was extended 60 days later and you have another two weeks before you meet with the person you *might* be working for. If you meet on May 12, you'll probably start working on June 1 and get paid for the first time on June 15. Maybe.

This time span is not atypical. And Haan Condominiums thinks, "We're really filling this position quickly!" Just a note of warning: Be prepared to wait a long time for companies to grind through the process. No matter how great you are, there is a lot of decision-making, a lot of paperwork to be handled. And travel schedules, vacations, conferences, etc., affect how quickly you get in to see someone and how quickly they move on their decisions (if they can even bring themselves to make decisions).

Good for you: During this whole adventure, you did not bug the company. There is no record here of lots of phone calls or letters in between the steps of this process. What is not shown here, of course, but on other records are the calls, letters, applications and interviews with a bunch of other companies all during this period. You would hardly put all your eggs in one condo. Keep up similar work with as many other potential employers as possible so that one—or more—will make the job offer.

"If you have a lucrative job offer, press one. If you have..."

One important logistical point: No one can or wants to sit by the phone all day, every day. Your best bet is to get an answering machine, leaving a professional-sounding message leaving no doubt to callers that they've reached the right number. Assure the caller that you'll be back in touch with them within 24 hours. Half the time the caller just wants to leave a message and doesn't need to speak with you, anyway.

If a prospective employer leaves a message that says an interview has been scheduled for 1:15 p.m. on Thursday, "if that's OK," you must call back and confirm one way or the other. Don't assume that silence on your part means you will be there. Otherwise, you'll show up at 1:15 p.m. and be given a surprised look. "You didn't call, so we assumed you couldn't make it." Oops.

Preparing for the interview: Role-playing and dress rehearsals

Getting the job interview is a lot of work. So much work, in fact, that you want to insure that the interview goes as well as possible. Which leads us to yet another round of self-examination and research.

I have two other books to recommend to you—***Your First Interview*** and ***101 Great Answers to the Toughest Interview Questions.*** As you can imagine, there are a lot of details in these books that will help you prepare for and get through your first round of interviews. Both books identify some of the most frequently asked interview questions—questions that you should expect, and for which you should prepare answers before the interview. And, a book I mentioned earlier, ***The Smart Woman's Guide to***

Resumes and Job Hunting, also contains many pages of useful information. We'll look at some of those tips in this chapter and the next one in this book.

One of the most useful exercises you can do is to role-play job interviews with your friends. Choose friends who are also interviewing for jobs—they'll take the role-playing much more seriously than someone who isn't.

"I don't know. Ask me something else."

Think about answers to these important questions below. We'll come back to some of the ideas here in the next chapter where we talk about the actual interview.

1. "Tell me about yourself."

Developing a successful answer to this most common question requires some preparation. You need to create a speech of 250 to 350 words (roughly 60 to 90 seconds when spoken). What should this speech be like? Leave out personal information. The interviewer isn't interested in your traumatic appendectomy in sixth-grade. It should include five elements highly targeted to your work history or work style:

1. Brief introduction to *you*
2. Your key accomplishments
3. The key strengths demonstrated by these accomplishments
4. The importance of these strengths and accomplishments to your prospective employer
5. Where and how you see yourself developing in the position for which you are applying

Here is what a recent college graduate applying for an entry-level sales position might say:

"I've always been able to get along with different types of people. I think it's because I'm a good talker and an even better listener. When I began thinking seriously about what careers I'd be best suited for, I thought of sales almost immediately.

"That thought really stuck in my senior year of high school and during summers at college when I worked various part-time jobs at retail outlets because, unlike most of my friends, I actually *liked* dealing with the public.

"However, I also realized that retail had its limitations. I read about various sales positions and was particularly fascinated by what is usually described as consultative selling. I like the idea of going to a client that you've really done your homework on and showing him how your products can help him solve one of his nagging problems and then following through on that.

"I wrote one of the papers in my senior year on the subject of consultative selling, and that led me to begin looking for companies at which I could learn and refine the skills shared by people who've become more like account executives than run-of-the-mill salespeople.

"That led me to your company, Mr. Shannon. I find the prospect of working with companies to increase the energy efficiency of their installations an exciting one. I've also learned some things about your sales training programs, and they sound like they're on the cutting edge.

"I guess the only thing I find a little daunting about the prospect of working at Cogeneration, Inc., is selling that highly technical equipment without an engineering degree. By the way, what sort of support does your technical staff lend to the sales effort?"

I recommend that you memorize this speech. After all, you're virtually guaranteed to be asked it. What's important is that you come across as confident, enthusiastic and clear on how your skills match the job opening.

2. "Why do you want to work for our company?"

Flip answers such as, "I'm desperate. I've been looking for work for six months," won't do. But you knew that.

This is where your job-research skills come into play. What did you learn about this company from your friends, newspaper and magazine clippings and other information at the library? Have a set of short sentences in your head that you have rehearsed—"I'm impressed with the kinds of products you make. A good example is the color-coded office-filing systems you recently introduced."

You sly fox. You may have read a business-journal article that said the woman you're interviewing with came up with this idea. Well, don't get too obvious, but it certainly doesn't hurt to toss a little praise with some precision. Praise with a rifle (directed at one person or department) may have more of an impact than praise with a shotgun (directed at the whole company or industry).

3. "What can you bring to this position?"

As with a lot of these questions, the interviewers pretty much know the answer, they just want to hear what you'll say—or if you'll freeze up, stumble over your own words, say something really stupid, or all of the above.

What do you say? You summarize the information you shared with them from the resume. You remind them that you have so many semesters or months of doing this and that, you learned this, you increased sales for that, and you'll bring all these strengths and skills to their company. And, boy, are you eager to begin. Choose buzzwords like "performance" and "results."

Note the emphasis of this question. What can *you* do for *them*? This will be the emphasis of the whole interview, so be ready to show your stuff and let them know why they should take a risk by hiring you.

4. "What experience do you have that's directly related to this job opening?"

For the sake of argument, let's assume you have some experience that's directly related. Again, the resume may have already shown how you are a good fit for this position, but you have to "put it in your own words."

Bring in the experiences you have from different aspects of your life—summer jobs, classroom training, volunteer work, reading and research, etc. Weave them together so you appear to be a person who knows what you're talking about, someone who will not walk in the first day without a clue as to what's going on, someone who knows basic terms (brush up on key words, names, events, publications and issues in the industry so you can converse with some familiarity on the topic).

5. "What do you know about computers (sales/photography/etc.)?"

Again, your interviewer may know the answer to this question almost as well as you do, but he or she wants to hear what you have to say. This is really a version of the "what can you bring us" question above. Don't get bogged down in detail.

Gear all your answers to the knowledge the interviewer has, too. You would answer the question about computers differently with the marketing director than you would with the person who is in charge of the computer lab. We could assume that the answer to the lab person can be more technical and even shorter than the answer to the marketing person.

In this case, explain what computer programs you are familiar with and share a (brief!) anecdote of a program you wrote or a problem you solved recently. Then shut up.

Keep all your answers fairly short, by the way. An "A" answer can drop to a "C-" if you keep on and on.

6. "What kind of career do you want?"

"Heck, I don't know," you say. "I just want a job that allows me to work indoors."

Surely you've given this some thought. If you haven't, put this book down as soon as you've finished this sentence and think about it.

Well?! What did you decide? No one expects you to trace a career from the job offer at hand to the gold-watch-giving 40-some years from now, even if you could.

They are really asking because: 1) they want to see how you handle yourself when you get dumb, but important open-ended questions like this one; and 2) they are thinking about what else you might be doing at their company in the near and distant future.

Is sales what you want to do for the rest of your life? Do you want to be on the front lines all that time or do you want to manage others who are out there selling?

Do you want to move from writer to editor to publisher or do you always want to do the writing?

There's not a right or wrong answer to this one, really; it's more *how* you answer the question. You can even say things like, "At this point in my life, I'm frankly not sure what I will be doing in 10 or 20 years from now, but I am confident that it will be in chemistry (publishing/automotive design/sales)."

It's fair for you to ask at this point what career paths are available at the company.

7. "Are you familiar with our company?"

Yep, you say. Then you elaborate by stating one of the company's recent achievements. ("I've been following the acquisition of Miller Tool & Die in the business press. How's that going, by the way?")

You will be familiar to a degree, at least, because you did all that research. Nobody expects you to be Mr. Wizard, but they do expect you to know whether they make toasters or repossess sailboats.

8. "What do *you* want to know?"

You should be prepared with some questions for your interviewer—if not to get answers that you need, then to show your interest and curiosity for the company and job. In fact, you should have been interjecting your own questions throughout the interview (see more on this in the next chapter.)

If you truly don't have any unanswered issues, here are some general questions you may want to ask:

- Can you give me a written description of the position, the major activities it involves, and the results expected?
- Does this job usually lead to other positions at the company? Which ones?

- Can you tell me some of the particular skills or attributes that you want in the candidate for this position?
- Can you tell me a little bit about the people with whom I'll be working most closely?
- What do you like best about this company? Why?
- What is the company's ranking within the industry? Does this position represent a change from where it was a few years ago?
- What new products is the company considering introducing over the next year or two?
- Has the organization had any layoffs or reductions in its work force over the last couple of years? Are any others anticipated? Was *this* department affected? How much?
- Is the company considering entering any new markets during the next few years? Which ones?
- You say you are anticipating a growth rate of "x" percent over the next few years. Will this be accomplished internally or through acquisitions?

Don't, however, ask about vacation, sick pay, personal days, etc., with hiring managers. It will make it seem as if you are looking for a chance to get out of the office *before you even start*!

Don't forget to rehearse those off-the-cuff remarks

Think up other questions that you might be asked by a particular company representative. Tape-record or video the role-playing and listen to and look for your strengths and weaknesses, then redo the role-playing.

You want to end up in the middle of "He sounds like he memorized all the answers" and "He doesn't have any idea how to answer this question." You want, in other words, carefully rehearsed, spontaneous answers.

There's the phone. Mrs. Moore is calling to set up an interview.

Chapter Five

The Job Interview

Root Canals May Cost More, But They're Sometimes More Fun

A friend of mine once had a job interview where he thought he said all the right things. As he proceeded toward the door in preparation to leave, however, he noticed the eyes of the interviewer get wider. He puzzled over this for a mega-second until he opened the door and walked into the coat closet. If he can get a job (and he did) after such an embarrassing move, so can you.

No, interviews aren't like root canals. They can actually be great learning experiences. What bothers people the most is that they feel they are on stage in a play that will never end. They must dress a certain way, act a certain way, say just the right things and know all the answers. So, what's the problem?

Give 'em an academy-award-winning performance

You *are* on stage, in a sense. You are performing for a person who probably didn't know you before you came into the room—other than what was on your resume and application. You have 30 minutes to convince him or her that you are qualified for this job, better qualified than anyone.

No matter what your mother told you, never get to an interview on time. Get there early.

If the interview is in a place you've never been to before, do a dry run. Drive there earlier in the week to see where, exactly, the building is, where to park and where the entrance is. Figure out how much time you'll need to get there. If you *don't* do this, you can end up on the morning of the interview, trying to figure out the map, wondering how much it will cost to park and already bemoaning the fact that you're late.

It is very bad form, in fact, it is plain, downright stupid to be late for a job interview. You *could* still get the job, but I don't think *I'd* hire you. The philosophy of most job interviewers is if you can't figure out how to get there on time, how can you figure out the complexities of the job?

Arrive 15 minutes early. Take off your coat. Go to the rest room. Fix your hair. Adjust your clothing. Pop a breath mint in your mouth. Calm down.

Only then do you announce yourself to the receptionist and tell her whom you have an appointment with and when. You should be announcing your arrival no less than five minutes before, preferably 10 minutes.

If you are in an office where the interviewer's secretary or even the interviewer comes to get you in the lobby, keep the conversation to small talk about the weather or other neutral topics. Don't say anything negative, like "I had a lot of trouble finding this place" or "What's that smell?"

Appearance: Put your best foot forward

Remember this: Impressions are being formed quicker than you can imagine. Just as you are sizing up the person escorting you (nice outfit, bad breath, nervous tic), he or she is doing the same with you. Don't offer any ammunition. That doesn't mean you freeze into a noncommittal zombie. It just means that you are very careful what you say and do. If you laugh nervously every time you turn a corner, or you are in such a state of excitement that you keep going the wrong way, it's eyebrow-raising time.

The interviewer is bound to ask the other person what kind of impression you made. If he or she says, "Kind of weird. She had this nervous laugh that drove me nuts," it will place a cloud over your application. Even though he knows you have every right to be nervous, he won't permit it to be shown.

You've all heard and read a lot about "dress for success." If you're just finishing college, you (and especially your parents) probably don't have a lot of money to throw at the local clothing stores. A very small number of outfits and accessories are in order, however.

Nobody at the big corporate headquarters dresses like college kids and they don't expect you to, either. You don't need tons of outfits and you may even be able to share clothing and accessories with friends, but you must show up in a complete outfit that looks good.

The man (and woman) in the gray flannel suit

Shine your shoes. And iron your shirts (or pay someone to wash and iron them professionally, at least for the interviews). Make sure spots and stains aren't visible.

Choose conservative clothes. No wild ties for men. No sports coats. Stick with suits. Dark colors. White or blue shirts. Get help if you're not comfortable dressing yourself.

For women, less is more, at least when it comes to jewelry, make-up and perfume. Don't overwhelm them with any of the above. Don't wear anything that makes noise or makes people go "sniff, sniff." Daytime make-up shouldn't be the same you might wear on Saturday nights, either. Tone it down.

A rule for men and for women: Don't wear anything that stands out more than you do. You want to be remembered among 55 applicants as "the woman who was ready with good answers to some tough questions," not as "the woman who was wearing that chartreuse paisley scarf."

Dress in clothes you are comfortable in. If the outfit is new, wear it somewhere else first; never try to go to an interview in something you've never worn before. You'll find yourself tugging at the sleeves or continually fixing something until the interviewer will want to get out of her chair, come across the room and either slap you silly or tie your scarf *tightly* around your neck.

I'll shake your hand as soon as I find a place for this suitcase

Other than a coat in the cooler months, bring only a folder with you and, for women, a reasonably sized purse. Try to avoid too much "stuff." Hang your coat, if possible, before you get to the interview so there are fewer things to mess with and distract you. Try to avoid being remembered for the quantity of stuff you brought rather than the quality of stuff you are made of.

The folder should be one of those kind you buy at a stationery store where an 8½ x 11 lined pad is on one side and a couple of pockets are on the other. The folder itself is a cordovan or black vinyl (or leather, if your trust fund just kicked in). Place a couple of resumes in the pockets and a couple of pens (that you know will write).

Use the pad in the folder during the interview to jot down information shared by the interviewer. Take some notes, even if it's only things like, "Don't forget to fix the cat tomorrow," so the interviewer thinks she's saying something important and interesting.

"How 'bout them Cubbies?"

Interviews usually begin with a limited amount of small talk, again confined to the weather, sports, some national event, etc. Without compromising your principles, refrain from voicing your opinions on politics, religion and other controversial topics. Even though the interviewer may agree with you, she may still find it inappropriate for you to voice your opinion on abortion or the President.

If the interviewer makes a statement that could draw you into such a discussion, give it your best noncommittal smile and avoid the fray. It may be a test to see what you'll do, but it's probably just the interviewer's opinions coming on loud and strong. If the interviewer persists, say, "I'd rather discuss the job opening," then immediately follow it up with a specific question about the job.

Otherwise, after a few minutes, the discussion will come around to why you are there. Throughout the interview, be sure to be asking questions. Don't sit quietly while the interviewer goes on and on about the company and the department and the position. Get your questions in as you go along. Be sure that some of them show you have an idea of what's going on. There's a mighty big difference between "Just what does this company do, anyway?" and "How will the cut in the defense budget affect your plant in Cleveland?"

Coming up with the latter question really didn't take much more effort than coming up with the first one. You know that you did some reading at the library and talked to a few people and read the company's own literature and you combined that with a basic knowledge of current events.

"What flavors of Jell-O do they carry in the cafeteria?"

Bring with you a set of questions that you want to have answered by the end of the interview. Have them jotted down on the pad and work your way through them as the interview progresses. If you get to the end where the interviewer asks if you have any more questions, and you haven't finished your list, then, by all means, do so.

If you don't ask questions, you will appear disinterested in the job. The interviewer may even think you aren't all that bright if you just sit there and don't come forward on your own. Remember, they are looking for someone who is a self-starter, someone who is a little assertive.

Now, there are questions and there are questions. We went over some of the basic ones at the end of the last chapter, and my books, ***Your First Interview*** and ***101 Great Answers to the Toughest Interview Questions*** give you—well—at least 101 more. But what we didn't discuss yet are the questions that the interviewer has no right to ask.

"You're the best-dressed bigot I've ever seen"

You probably know a lot of them. He can't ask you, for example, what religious faith you profess, or what political party you're a member of. Nor can he probe into your racial and ethnic background without giving you reasons to think he is prejudiced and is simply determining that you are, indeed, a member of the "wrong" group.

While it may be said innocently, the comment, "That's an interesting name. Is that Swedish?" can be intruding into "no-no" areas just as much as, "Hispanic, huh? You're the first of your kind to interview for this sales job." No amount of sincere smiling on his part will excuse a tasteless and ethnically insensitive *faux pas*.

If, after the position is filled by someone else, you have any reason to believe you were turned down for it because of your gender, race, religious faith, ethnic origin, etc., raise a fuss. (To get advice on how to initiate such a complaint, contact an attorney or talk to the appropriate civil-rights group in your hometown, such as the National Organization of Women, the B'nai B'rith or the NAACP.)

Of course, you have no more right as the interviewee to ask the interviewer about his or her background. Besides, you're there to get a job, not compile the U.S. census.

Interviewers also have no business asking you your marital status, whether you have children, whether you are or expect to become pregnant, whether you intend to work after you have your first child and other questions of this kind.

It doesn't mean you can't bring up in the conversation the fact that you have a spouse or imminent wedding plans. You don't have to hide your personal life; you just have to be aware that you shouldn't be discriminated against because of it.

In a sense, the company is being interviewed at the same time you are being interviewed. If you don't like the type of questions the interviewer is asking (e.g., he is dwelling on the origin of your surname), then you're not going to be happy working for him. In addition, your questions demand straightforward, complete answers. If you get the runaround, it means either that the interviewer doesn't know the answers, and is too embarrassed to say so, or that he won't tell you. In either case, it's a danger signal.

Let your fantasies be your guide

You need to visualize yourself in the company. Can you work for this person? Can you do the work he or she is describing? Are there major objections to working here? If so, can they be worked out—or do you want to work them out? What will happen if you're offered a job?

You may not, of course, interview with your prospective boss at all, at least not for the first interview. Entry-level jobs especially are often conducted by interviewers in the human resources office.

The human resources interviewer you meet with will probably be interviewing all applicants for the same job, unless they are hiring, say, five people to do the same thing; in that case, he or she may be sharing the interview load with one or two others in the human resources department.

Human resources people are responsible for matching applicants with job descriptions. Prospective employees who don't meet the minimum qualifications don't get considered. The interviewers also act as a filter in other ways: If they are conducting the first interviews, they sort out the people who don't seem appropriate and they also sort out those who don't appear to be of the personality and mind-set to work with the person who will be the supervisor.

On the other hand, if the human resources person is impressed with the applicant, he or she will highlight the application and see if there isn't a fit somewhere else in the corporation. (Remember that when you are interviewing: You may not get this job, for all kinds of reasons, but you might make such a good impression that the interviewer recommends you for another job within the company—or even suggests you talk with a buddy over at some other corporation.)

To give you an idea of what you can be up against, numbers-wise, here's a typical breakdown for a single job opening: The company runs an ad and receives 125 applications in the human resources office. Human resources people sift through the pile and select the top 15. (Of the remaining 110, we can assume that some were simply not qualified, some were highly overqualified, some sent in their resumes on pink paper (yes, I am obsessed with that memory) and the rest met the minimum education and experience requirements, but the top 15 were simply "better."

The 15 then go to the future supervisor who selects five for interviews. They're chosen on an objective basis (they write well, they have solid experience that matches what is needed for this job and a good, applicable college degree) and, perhaps, on a subjective basis (they graduated from a prestigious institution, they are involved in activities the screener approves of, they have or do not have certain racial/gender/ethnic characteristics).

We can only hope that the screener leaned most heavily on the objective side and that he or she really didn't choose someone because they were female or because they were white or because they attended the "right" college. Short of torture or truth serum, however, we'll never know.

So. From 125 to 15 to 5 to...1. Look at it this way: Somebody's got to be that one. Why not you?

Prior to any interview, as long as your application has met certain basic criteria (including no jelly stains on the front), you may be called in to take some preliminary tests.

Anticipate being tested throughout the whole process of getting a job—and even afterward. What you are being tested for may be based partly on the type of business, of course, and it may also reflect the biases of the human resources department or even the CEO.

Personality tests ("When you enter a crowded room, do you: a) offer your hand to the first person you see; b) wait for someone to introduce him/herself to you; or c) head for the bar), general knowledge tests ("How did Mussolini die?") and math tests ("If you had three live chickens and your friend had two live chickens, how many live chickens would you have?") will be among the most common.

One major reason for the testing, too, is to see if you've got many smarts. No one expects you to get all the math questions right or to know everything there is to know about history and current events or even to come up with all the "right" answers in the personality tests. But they do watch for certain patterns.

It would be pretty unusual for someone in sales or marketing to keep checking off the answers that show him or her to be a quiet person. A writer or computer programmer, on the other hand, might not be expected to be so gregarious, although it wouldn't count against them.

You may also be asked to complete sentences, such as "My mother ____________" or "When I am depressed, I ____________." (Avoid mentioning the use of sharp objects.) People do not go into the human-resources field "because it's just so much fun."

In fact, when you are interviewing, filling out applications, talking on the phone with someone you don't know, watch the "humor." Even mild jokes have a way of wearing on the other person, especially if they are trying to get their job done and you keep "interrupting" with something funny. Nervousness brings this out in people.

Do the following: Smile a lot. Make eye contact. Give a firm, but not bone-crushing, handshake. Provide occasional thoughtful gazes. Sit upright. In sum, do all those things your mother has told you to do for years.

You may be offered coffee or something to drink. Be very, very careful here. Feel free to accept; just make sure you place the cup or glass well away from where you are sitting so that you don't knock it over. You don't have to drink it all, but it helps make you look relaxed if you are sitting comfortably, smiling across the desk at the interviewer, raising a cup of coffee to your lips.

Lunch interviews

There's good news and bad news accompanying the news that you have a lunch interview. The good news (the only good news, probably) is that you're getting a free lunch. The bad news is that you must be just as great as you would be in an office and you've got to handle a knife and fork, as well.

If you have the time, and you know where you'll be having lunch, you might even go there with a friend a couple of days before to study the menu—and eat, of course. Then when you have the lunch interview, you'll not read every line of the menu while trying to explain why you love math.

Do your eating and drinking in slow motion. No sudden movements, no quick reaches for anything. Take your time, and your water goblet will be your friend, not an enemy that decides to pour itself in your interviewer's lap. Not only will you be listening extra hard, you will be making even more eye contact than is legal during lunch, so be especially careful that you don't shove your sleeve into the bowl of thousand island dressing.

Don't order anything harder than iced-tea. Even if the interviewer gets a glass of wine, stick with the soft stuff. Don't take any chances. Most people these days do not drink during a daytime business engagement, despite the legends you have heard about the three-martini lunches.

Avoid food that fights back

Try to order food that isn't messy or complicated. This may be the first meal you've ever had where the food isn't discussed (or even hardly touched), but remember why you're there: To get a job, not be a restaurant critic. (Of course, if the job is being a restaurant critic, then, by all means, emote away.)

A salad may be easier to manage than soup. Or a thick soup like chili may be easier than a more liquid one. You decide.

Main courses that require a lot of attention should be avoided because you will be trying to finagle something with two pieces of silverware just as he asks you, "Why do you want to work for our company?" Lobster, peel-and-eat shrimp, spaghetti, even French onion soup may be wise to pass up. Imagine the awkward moment as your interviewer waits for your reply, while you attempt to disengage the melted cheese that is still connecting your mouth to your soup bowl.

This may be a trick interview in that the interviewer wants to see how you conduct yourself in just such a situation. After all, if he hires you, you may have to take clients to lunch or go with him on occasion and he doesn't want to hire people who constantly draw attention to themselves by knocking things over or dropping food or—heaven forbid—talking with their mouths full. Use your napkin often. It's pretty disconcerting for the interviewer to take you seriously if there is a noodle hanging from your chin.

Take small bites—you're going to be doing a lot of talking, remember—and don't expect to finish your plate.

Keep the cost of the meal to a reasonable level. If he orders the $8.95 entree, keep yours there—or lower. Ask what he recommends, if you don't know the restaurant. (If this is beginning to sound like you're his "date," well, in a sense, you are. Guys, get used to it.) Unless he insists he's going to have dessert, pass on it. First, it's just more food to fight with while you're trying to tell him about your internship in Thailand, and, second, it drives up the bill.

A cup of after-lunch coffee is restful and recommended, if you are a coffee drinker. The table has been cleared off and you can now really concentrate on the interview.

Body language is as important at the luncheon interview as it is in any other interview situation. Just because you're in a restaurant, don't get so relaxed that you lean back in your chair and forget you're "on stage." Watch how you sit, what you do with your hands (use them for expressing yourself but keep them clutched to the silverware or in your lap most of the time) and where you put your feet. (Try not to kick the interviewer under the table even one time. More than once is considered grounds for not being offered dessert—or the job.)

Skip the bit about what I do. How much do I make?

Whether your interviewer is discussing salary over the celery or she brings up the question in the office, it's going to come up sometime in the interview process. Depending on how the job is advertised, the salary range may already have been posted, so you, at least, will know that you will end up between, say, $18,000 and $22,000.

Most of the time, however, the salary issue will be The Big Secret of the interview. Chances are, in fact, the interviewer will avoid telling you what the salary is, but will rather ask *you* what salary you require.

The wisest strategy for you is to first convince the interviewer that she and her company cannot survive any longer without you. Once you've established that, other issues—like salary—become more negotiable. If you play your cards too early—or you express an excessive amount of interest in salary too soon into the discussion—you may create a roadblock to further consideration.

For example, you've determined that you would not accept the position for any less than $28,000. You reveal that to your interviewer after a couple of questions. She then informs you that they had targeted a maximum of $25,000 for the position. Instead of exploring further and discovering that you have such a unique set of skills and experience that the company would consider a higher salary, she's just determined that you are probably not a match for the job and is not listening to another word you say.

Try to avoid salary discussions until you have a complete understanding of the job, and the interviewer has a clear picture of you. Once that's been established, try to avoid giving a specific requirement—until you've been given an offer. If pressed, you might say, "I'd expect to be paid a fair amount for this area of the country and for my level of experience—which would be somewhere between $28,000 and $35,000. You have, of course, already researched compensation levels for this particular position, so your figures shouldn't come as a shock to your interviewer. Don't include a figure in your range that is lower than you would accept.

Ideally, you would find out what the proposed salary or salary range is before you are asked to give your requirements. In that case, you can simply say, "It looks as if your salary range would meet my requirements." And then move on to other discussion opportunities that allow you to show off your stellar qualities.

Whatever you do, don't comment on the answer. No whistles if it's higher than expected. No vulgarisms if lower. Dutifully write it down on the pad.

Remember that salaries are based on a lot of factors that you may not be aware of. If you are a Level A-12 employee, you will be making, within a couple thousand dollars, what every other A-12 employee in the company is making. The longer on the job and/or the better you do the job, the more you will get. There will be a ceiling for each job, however, as long as it's classified an A-12. To make more, you've got to move up to an A-*13*.

I'm telling you all this at this point so that you know, when the interviewer says, "I can't pay you any more than that because it's a Level A-12 job," he may actually be telling the truth.

Concluding the interview

How does the interview end? Graciously, with handshakes and smiles and thank-you's all around, you hope. Leave with no more flurry and fuss and gathering of huge amounts of "stuff" than when you came in.

Will you be offered the job at this time? Very doubtful. Will you be asked to return for a second interview ("I'd like you to come back to meet with the assistant director, Mr. Tarkitoff")? Possibly. It's certainly a good sign. After all, if you bombed or the interviewer determined that you were unsuitable for any of 100 reasons, he wouldn't be setting up a second interview.

In the excitement of leaving, and of discussing a second interview, find out who does what next. Probably Tarkitoff's secretary will call you to set up an appointment, but they may want to set up something right then and there. For that reason, have your calendar with you (tucked in a pocket of the folder) so you can take care of it on the spot.

Whatever you do, don't leave with a vague idea of what happens next if another appointment is to be scheduled. Otherwise, you'll end up trying to reach a secretary whose name you don't know and it will all be a big nuisance.

If the interviewer doesn't mention another appointment, it doesn't mean that you are out of the picture, however. It could mean that he has six more people to interview, at least, and he doesn't want to move too quickly before he sees all of them.

You'll never get away from grade cards

Of the ones he's interviewed already, including you, however, he probably has placed you in an A, B or C category. It's just like it sounds. The Cs are dead meat. The Bs are maybes, if the As—the top choices—refuse, die or self-explode. Of course, you can move from one to another category depending on what you do after the interview, what you do at the second interview and whether or not the CEO's daughter wants the job.

Tell the interviewer you appreciated his time and that you look forward to hearing from him soon. You can summarize your interest in the job by telling him, too, that you would be delighted to be chosen to work at his company and that you believe your qualifications and interests would be a good match for the company's needs. Say it quickly, be direct about it, then move on to the final small talk. ("So, are they predicting any more snow for tonight?")

Don't forget to thank the secretary and any other people who were involved who are in the immediate area. Shake their hands, too. Bond.

When you get to your car, make some quick notes on the interview: Names, personal information they revealed, information about the job you have learned (not just salary, but duties, travel possibilities, the set-up of the department, etc.).

When you get back to your computer, enter this data, in much greater detail, in the file you're keeping on this company.

"So, is your husband still in San Quentin?"

I learned a trick many, many years ago from the father of one of my friends. He was a salesman. Whenever he was in an office waiting to see the boss, he'd strike up a conversation with the others working there. They would talk, of course, about their families, events, and so forth for a few minutes each time he came to visit. He'd do the same with the boss.

As soon as he got back to his car, he'd whip out his tape recorder and rapid-fire record information on everyone: "Dorothy, the secretary: Dorothy's son is at Penn State, majoring in agronomy. He broke his leg skiing last week in Vermont. Bill the bookkeeper: Bill was elected president of the PTA at the elementary school where his twins go. His wife is pregnant."

You guessed it. The next time he came to call, he'd play the tape back to himself in the car just before he went into the office. As he walked in, he'd spot Dorothy and ask, jovially, "Dorothy, how's your son's leg? Well, hello, Bill. Say, how's the PTA business?" And on and on and on. The applause—and the sales—never stopped.

But I'm getting ahead of myself. You don't dare return for a second interview until you've sent a thank-you note for the first one. Whether it's a human resources person or the director of sales, you send a note, thanking the person for the opportunity (a good word) to interview with them for the position. (Keep your ego in check—they may not remember you all that well, especially if you were Number 23 out of 30 for five customer-service positions.)

These sincerely written and heartfelt letters will, of course, be on your computer where you will insert the correct name, address and job title each time. Done.

Chapter Six

The Job Offer—and Acceptance

"Mom, Guess What? I Got the Job! Can I Borrow Five Hundred Bucks?"

Yikes! They offered the job. Now what?

Suddenly, you have to make some hard decisions. Here you've been concentrating on researching the companies, getting the right wardrobe together, filling out applications, doing countless interviews and—*it paid off!*

Calm down. This isn't the *beginning* of the world any more than it's the end of it.

Very often, a job offer is made over the telephone by someone in human resources who has been told you are to be hired with a certain title, to report to a certain person, to start on a certain day at a certain salary. They will know that you have an application on file and that you've been interviewed one or more times.

You already know the job title, we presume, and the name of the supervisor. You probably have met that person and even interviewed with him or her. The starting date, unless it is predicated on your finishing school or some other factor, will probably be in a couple of weeks. And the salary should be a figure that falls within the range you should already be aware of.

You do not have to say yes or no right there on the phone. Of course, there's no point in stalling if you've taken another job or it's one of those over-my-dead-body-will-I-work-for-this-company situations. Just thank them, tell them that you are no longer available. That should end that.

If you are interested, however, the fun begins. Perhaps this is the only job offer you've received and no more are on the horizon. Maybe you've been given one or two more, or you know for sure you are one of three finalists for that chemist's job over at Frankstine Laboratories.

In the case that you have more than one job offer to choose from, tell the person that you will have to let him or her know. Make sure you have all the information written down—start date, salary, etc.—and confirm when you must respond.

Eenie-meenie-miney-mo, which job should go?

Now comes the hard part. Which job should you take? Salary is a consideration, of course, but it's only one of many and, in the whole scheme of life, it really isn't the most important one. Besides, if you have two or three job offers and you are coming right out of college, there probably isn't much difference in the salaries anyway.

In that case, look at the other factors: What are your prospective bosses like? Where are the jobs located—within an easy commute, or would you have to move for any of them? How much travel is involved? What opportunities are there for advancement within the departments or within the companies? What are your duties at each job? What's your overall gut reaction to the jobs?

It could be that you are being asked to do something you are unhappy about. Many companies today, for example, require all new employees to be tested for drug use. This could bother you because you do use drugs or it could bother you because you feel it is in violation of the trust between you and your employer. In any case, you won't have a choice. Either you agree to be tested or you won't get the job. (The job offer is made, by the way, contingent on a couple of things: That your references check out and that you come up "negative" on the drug test.)

With the issue of substance abuse in the work force being such a concern these days, you may find that most companies require drug testing for all new employees. You should be prepared to confront this in your job search.

Bad vibes: Could it be the employee torture chamber?

If you have negative vibes, what's wrong? You could feel uncertain because one job is a 45-minute commute and the other is 7-minutes from your house. If you like the first job better for all kinds of other reasons, is it worth taking in spite of the commute? (Or can you move?)

What about the job itself? Maybe you've got negative feelings because the one boss is ready to turn you loose on the very kind of work you love and the other boss is putting you in an assembly-line kind of atmosphere.

Maybe it's because you really love the challenges at one job, but you don't think you'll get along with the boss. But, at the other place, you really like the woman who would be your supervisor, but the work is not so exciting.

Do it the old-fashioned way: Write down the pros and cons on a piece of paper and decide how "big" the pros and the cons are. If you can learn to live with a longer commute because the job itself is much more exciting, you say the commute is "a small con" and the job itself is a "big pro."

A part of me wants to say to you, "This is your first job. Take almost anything just to get the experience. Look upon it as a learning experience, one that will provide you with powerful tools for future jobs."

That's all true, you know. Face it: If your fabled first job was as a semi-trailer driver on cross-country runs, you'd learn independence, how to handle personal relationships and how to meet deadlines, to say nothing of where the best peach cobbler is between Memphis and Ft. Wayne.

Overall, what job will give you the most satisfaction? Even if you're looking at only one offer, this process of examining the pros and cons should help you pinpoint your biggest priorities and determine how "right" a particular job is for you.

Now we get to the negotiating. Let's say you have settled on two jobs that are similar enough in the important areas (job description, location, etc.) that you really could be happy at either place. What you have to determine now is how much are you worth to the company.

Don't look now, but there are 6,000 more applicants standing behind you

Remember this: Ross Perot, you aren't. The company is not going to fall over backwards upping its salary figure significantly because you might go elsewhere. After all, you are relatively inexperienced and you resemble a ton of other people out there. You don't have, in other words, a lot to negotiate from. So don't try to call the bluff of the company be demanding a lot more money—just because you got an offer.

But don't under-sell yourself, either. You should consider whether the salary is indeed acceptable to you—and if it isn't, then you have nothing to lose by negotiating a reasonable increase.

Weighing the benefits package

We're not just talking salary here. We're looking at the whole benefits package. Maybe getting another couple of thousand dollars tacked on to the death and dismemberment policy isn't your concern, but you should look at everything you are offered here.

First, of course, you've got to find out what you have coming to you. Each company's package will help determine which one you go for, should you have a choice. You need to look at health insurance, dental insurance, life insurance, vacations, sick leave, pre-tax amounts you can set aside for health and childcare costs, travel benefits (if any), company vehicles and on and on.

The human resources people are best-equipped to provide you, in writing, with everything you need to consider. Ask them for details when they offer you the job. Don't settle for vague details ("well, we have a health plan but I don't have the information right here"). Get the information.

A poor health plan (from the employee's point of view) could mean a big difference in your out-of-pocket expenses. You will have a certain amount deducted from each check to cover the basic costs and then you need to look at how much you have to pay (a yearly deductible plus a certain percentage of the costs above the deductible).

If the plan costs you, as a single person, $8 a pay period but it has an $800 deductible, it won't be as attractive as one that costs you $20 a pay period but has a $150 deductible.

Get all the figures on all the benefits and consider them carefully. A fantastic benefits package (health insurance paid by the company, four weeks of vacation, two weeks of sick time, a company car, tuition reimbursement—and free lunch on your birthday) and a smaller salary may be more attractive than mediocre benefits and a larger salary.

Now I see why they call it "gross"

Figure up how much take-home pay you will have—you can get pretty close—to see what you will end up with in your pocket every other Friday.

If it's not enough, figure up how much is "enough" (actually, you should know this already). *Then* you're ready to negotiate. Don't ask for a figure in the sky just because it's more than they offered. If you know that you need $2,000 more a year to live a reasonable existence, then ask for $3,000 more. However, donpt approach the company with your financial woes. You should be petitioning for a higher salary because of the value you'll bring to the company.

If you ask for $3,000 more when $2,000 will do, you have some room for play. If you ask for $2,000, they may offer $1,000 and you suddenly realize that still isn't enough. Oops.

The negotiator figures that you are asking for more than you expect to get. That's how the game is played. You may end up with half, or $1,500. I'd say, if the job is good, take it.

Items like the insurances are not likely to be negotiable, although you may have options to choose from (lower or higher deductibles, etc.). Depending on the type of job, you may be able to get them to agree to provide you with other kinds of benefits, such as a six-month performance review (where you can expect to get a salary increase, provided you have done well) instead of waiting for 12 months.

Get it in writing

Make sure any agreements are in writing. Ask them to do so, if they don't provide you with a letter. The letter should include the start date, the job title, the beginning salary and the special arrangements (earlier performance review, etc.). Details of other arrangements, such as policies on company cars, should they give you one, will be written elsewhere.

Suppose you ask for something more and they say no, no, three thousand times no? Well, you tried. You can either take it or leave it. That depends on whether you have another job offer at hand or expect to, and whether the experience the job will provide you is worth it to you. While you don't want them to hire you under such pressure, as it will make you resentful, you may be forced to take the original offer, with no "extras," and go on from there.

That's not all bad. At least you showed them you were interested in negotiating and that you were willing to go along when you found out you couldn't do anything else. You may just have laid a little guilt on them, especially when you show them you are even better than they expected, and they will look even more favorably upon you when the next review comes up.

Maintaining good relationships

It is important to remember throughout this delicate time between the job offer(s) and acceptance to maintain good relationships with absolutely everyone. Return phone calls, be polite, send letters, make yourself available for meetings and so forth. Don't burn any bridges. The job you *don't* take this time may be the company you are going to work for two years from now. Or the person who would have been your boss there might just end up being your boss at the company you did go with.

And paper the town with thank-you notes and calls. Send thank-you's to the people who thought enough of you to offer you a job, even if they wouldn't meet your salary and you had to turn them down. And be sure and send thank-you's to the people who helped you get the job you did take. It would be very bad form for them to find out from someone else that, even though they called Fred

Barney over at Barney Manufacturing on your behalf, you didn't bother to tell them that you are the hottest, newest employee there. Mind your manners.

Once you have the job firmly in hand, but before you get in the throes of the first few days and weeks, send a short note to all the other people who were so supportive during your research/networking days. Tell them that you are pleased that you have been offered—and have accepted—the job as (job title) at (company name), starting on (date). Tell them you are so pleased to be joining the ranks of this company and that you look forward with great excitement to beginning your work. Thank them for all their good advice.

They may have done nothing more than listen to you babble on the phone three months ago and suggested you do something obvious that you had already done, but you thought enough of them to contact them in the first place so they must be important—and perhaps useful in future.

In case you thought you had some spare time

You probably don't have the leisure of devoting all of your time between the acceptance of the job and the first day at work to preparing for the job, but there are several things you should do to make your first job staff off right.

- Ask your future boss for as much information about the company, the department you will be working in, the industry—in printed form or on computer disk—as they are willing to throw at you. You may not be able to read it all, but you will impress your boss with your request and you will learn a lot from what he or she gives you.

  At the least, read through the most important articles or documents and briefly scan the rest.

Definitely read thoroughly anything that was specifically noted by the boss. Make a few notes on what you've read, including any questions you have.

- Also ask for several back issues of the employee newsletter, if you haven't already seen them. The articles will provide information on what the employees are doing and, very importantly, what they have done to be recognized and honored by the company.
- Otherwise, psych yourself up to working full-time. ("You mean, I don't get off in the summer? But I've always been off in the summer!")
- Get your wardrobe ready. You should have asked about or read about your company's dress code during the interview process. Plan two weeks' worth of outfits, in accordance with the acceptable standards. That doesn't mean you have to own 10 of everything. You can wear some of the items more than once, but you need to plan your accessories so that it *looks* like you have 10 different outfits.

  Depending on the company and the job, there is a certain tolerance given to young people who are entering the work force straight from college. Everyone knows you didn't wear corporate attire *ever*; on the other hand, don't ever abuse that sympathy by wearing something that's not appropriate for your new workplace.
- Ask for a copy of the employee handbook, if they'll give you one before you actually begin working, so that you can read through it to find out what everyone is expected to do/not to do.

  There probably won't be a lot of surprises, but it's good to know all the little policies so that you don't do something later on because you failed to read the book. Employee handbooks will cover a myriad of areas, from how to apply for other jobs within the company to vacation policies (how many days you get, how soon you must ask for a vacation, etc.) to cafeteria hours.

The books are usually loose-leaf so that changes and additions can be made frequently, and, in most companies, all employees are given a copy.

- Human resources may give you forms to fill out during this time period, but you'll probably be handed them on the first day (see the next chapter).
- Talk to yourself. I personally think it's important to say to yourself before you take a new job or begin any new, major task in your life: "I'm really going to do the best I can, but I will make mistakes. I'll try to avoid mistakes, but I will make them."

  And you will make mistakes. Nobody gets a 4.0 in the corporate world. There are two certainties: 1) You'll make some errors. 2) You'll learn from those errors.
- Develop some habits that will help you in your new job. If it's in the financial sector, for example, and your favorite TV shows are all on MTV, you don't have to drop the music videos, but add "Wall Street Week" and similar shows to your line-up, even if you have to tape them and watch them at a different time.

  Subscribe, if you can afford it, to certain magazines that are the standard-bearers in the industry you are now joining. If you can't subscribe, set up a weekly time to go to the public library (or company library) and read them.

Keeping up with trends, issues, personalities, etc. is very important. And it gives you something to talk about when you're in the elevator with the CEO.

Take care of number one

And, finally, treat yourself to something. You deserve it. Buy yourself a little something for your new desk. It may cost less than five bucks, but make this your "good luck piece" and take it with you from job to job.

And, years from now, you can look at it and think, "Can you believe I bought that before I went to work at my first job?"

Chapter Seven

Your First Job

Now That You've Got It, What Do You Do With It?

Take a deep breath, heave a sigh, open the door of the great big building full of employed adults and walk inside. Welcome to your first job.

No matter whether you've been out of college for two days or you're starting your first job after raising four children or you're entering the work force fresh from high school, the process can be a little intimidating.

It may, in fact, remind you of moving to another town and being the new kid in the school where everyone else knows everyone else and they all stare at you as you enter the room. You could have sworn you were wearing a big "Kick me!" sign.

It's not that bad. Really. Actually, it's quite exciting. If you've done even half of what I told you to do in the earlier chapters, you're pretty much in control of your situation. You know the names and faces of a few of the people already working here, you are familiar with the company history and philosophy, you're ready to put your skills to work and, most importantly, you have memorized the hours the cafeteria is open.

You're wearing one of your first 10 outfits and, of course, you've worn it before so you won't be going through that awful self-conscious tugging-and-pulling routine that will make them wonder why they hired you. You have arrived five minutes ahead of time and you go to the room you were told to go.

No doubt you've been told to report to human resources so you can spend the first six months of your job filling out forms. They already have a file folder on you that contains your resume, application and any scores of tests you've taken so far. Your employee number and job title may well be on that crisp, typed file label (color-coded to your department, of course). You belong.

You will be given forms to fill out regarding your choice of benefits, tax information and basic personal information in case the computer blows up and they must notify your "next of kin" whose first heart-felt words will no doubt be, "How much insurance did he take out?"

Again, if you've done your homework, you'll be somewhat familiar with the benefits package, but take your time to read it over. Once you sign the forms, you may not be able to make any changes except once a year, usually in November, when everyone is given a chance to make other selections during the "open season." (If that makes you feel like a deer caught in the gun sights of the insurance companies, hey, you've about got it right.)

There are no dumb questions. Ask whatever you need to ask of the person in charge of the benefits programs. This is your money. Some benefits are provided by the company at no charge to you; others will cost you something out of each paycheck, but the forms and/or the person helping you will tell you how much. It may be a percentage, so have a small calculator in your briefcase (you've now graduated from a folder to a real briefcase).

Once you've selected all the benefits and your withholding-tax category (number of dependents), you should be able to find out what your approximate net income will be. It will give you a running start on the "sticker shock."

Find out, too, when the benefits really begin. Most health insurance plans, for example, don't kick in for at least 30 days so you are either taking a risk for a month or so, or you take out a temporary policy to cover yourself. (When you transfer from one plan to the other, you can usually get a "grace period"—you pay for it, of course—long enough to keep you covered. To be safe, check on this.)

Payday

Most companies pay every two weeks, usually on a Friday or on certain days of the month (the 1st and the 15th are popular selections).

Ask when your first check will be. Let's say you start on Monday, May 1. Friday, May 12, will probably be when you get your first check. But it might not be until Friday, May 19. Your first check might be for the regular two-week period, but the first time it might just cover one week.

There's a chance the existing employees will get checks a few days after you arrive, but you won't since you didn't actually work any days during the pay period covered.

Some companies pay once a month, but this is the exception. Should you have failed to determine this before you showed up for work, you may be in for a rude shock to find out that you can't expect to have a check for a full 30 days. That's where the "Mom, can I have 500 bucks?" comes in.

OK, so I work here for 50 years, then I...

Pension and retirement plans may now seem like so much esoteric gobbledygook, but you want to read this information carefully. Decide on what you can afford now to do, if given an option as to how much money you can set aside, remembering that some companies may match some or all of what you are putting aside.

There may also be profit-sharing plans where you actually share in the profits of the company, provided there are any, once or twice a year. Don't understand it all? Read the materials and ask lots of questions.

Setting aside pre-tax money to cover health and child-care expenses is relatively new, but it can be a major benefit. Here's how it works: You calculate how much you expect your health care to cost you during the period in question (probably the remainder of the calendar year). This doesn't count the money that is deducted from your paycheck to pay for your health insurance. The costs I am referring to here are the checks you have to write the doctor, hospital and pharmacy for any care you are receiving that is not covered by insurance.

Remember, you are selecting a certain amount for a deductible, and that option will determine which plan you have chosen (and, consequently, how much is taken out of your check). Typically, you will have two or three options.

If your deductible is, say, $150, you might want to set aside that amount in the pre-tax category. That means that, when you go see your doctor and the insurance will not cover it (or you haven't yet reached your deductible), and the doctor charges you $35 for the visit, you have to fork over the whole $35. However, if you have money set aside in the pre-tax account, you can pay the doctor, file for a reimbursement and get your $35 back.

Because it's "pre-tax," it means that you don't pay tax on that money so the money is "worth" more. If you earned $35, and taxes were taken out, you would end up with something less than $35. This way, the money you earned—and set aside in this account—is used to pay for these expenses. Depending on your tax bracket, you could have maybe 28 percent more money available to you to pay for the medical costs you would have to pay for anyway.

The one down side is that this money, if not spent, is not returnable to you. Poof. It's gone. Plan carefully, then, on how much you want to have withheld pre-tax. If you are near the end of the period and you don't expect to use up the rest, consider buying another pair of eyeglasses or getting contacts. Short of ordering a new set of toes, there's not much else you can do if you've overcalculated.

Back to class...orientation class, that is

You may be going through this whole paperwork process all alone, stuck in some cubbyhole in the human resources department, or you might be in a room with a lot of other new employees.

The bigger the company, the more likely that you'll have an orientation period that lasts from one day to one week. During this time, you'll be taken through the paces—the company history, the role of the company in the industry, greetings by top management and all the categories of employee life as outlined by the employee handbook. In fact, this is where you receive the employee handbook, if there is one, and you will be given ample time to ask questions about any of the topics.

Overall, the class is intended to explain to you the "corporate culture" of the company. As you know by now, different companies operate in different ways. From sociology class, we tend to think of cultures as belonging to groups of people who have modes of behavior, styles of dress and philosophies in common. Corporations are their own such groups. Certain companies expect, even demand, that their employees dress a certain way. Men might be required to wear suits, not sports coats, and the suits might have to be dark shades of gray and blue, not browns. Other companies might not care if their male employees wear suit coats at all, even though the nature of the work is about the same as at the first company.

In some companies, senior management rarely interacts with staff members; in others, there may be a friendly interchange of conversations and ideas.

What are they eating back in tourist class?

The company cafeteria is a good indicator of how management and staff view themselves. If there are reserved sections for senior management, it's a different sort of company from one where vice presidents break bread with the guys from the mailroom.

Your orientation class will include not only those of you who are just entering the work force, but other new employees who are in mid-career. It's a good chance to get to know people from several different departments.

Tours of the physical plant are typical in the orientation classes, too, so you'll get a chance to get a good look at everything.

Even though you'll probably be spending most of the orientation time in the class, you'll be given a couple of hours, at least, to meet with your new boss and get introduced to the other people in the department.

You'll be shown to your desk and the assistant for the area will probably have a stack of supplies (pens, paper, etc.) already waiting for you. It's as exciting as the first day of school when you were a kid—and now you're getting paid for it!

Finally, orientation is over and you're now ready to sit down at your own desk. But, wait! Your boss has probably scheduled you to meet with several other people in the department as well as others in the company. Whom you meet with and how many people you meet with will depend partly on your job duties and on how much your boss wants you to jump right in and get to know the company.

Good bosses help you get established quickly. You must never forget that you are there to make your boss look good. Think about that: If you look good (i.e., you prepare great reports, you increase sales, etc.), you make the boss look good. ("Jane sure hired a winner!" is a comment that Jane doesn't mind "sharing" with you.) More on this later.

Good bosses want you to feel comfortable so you will produce that much more work that much faster. One way for your boss to do that is to introduce you to everyone so you'll start putting names and faces together and begin working with them immediately.

Did Chris have the green dress, the green eyes or the green hair?

If you are meeting with more than three people, no one expects you to remember everything that is being said, nor even to remember names and faces. That doesn't mean you shouldn't try; it just means that you shouldn't feel bad if you can't remember whether Sandy Munson is the head of Shipping or of Sales or even if Sandy is a male or female. At the end of a long day of smiling and meeting with people, you may not remember if *you* are male or female.

Get used to answering the same questions over and over. Where did you work before you came here? What was your major in college? How did you happen to come to work here? What are you going to be doing? Just keep on smiling.

Now, let's talk about something really interesting: *Me*

One way to impress the people you are meeting with and actually learn something in the process is to handle their questions quickly and politely, then turn the conversation around to them. We all love to talk about ourselves. Find out what they do at the company, how long they've been there and so on. Mix a lot of small talk and personal items in with these initial conversations. Ask about the people in the pictures on their desks. Comment on any art work or memorabilia they have in their offices.

There are some practical considerations here. First, after you've said where you went to school and that you've never held an honest job in your life, what else is there to say about yourself? You're no longer selling your vast experience as a boy scout troop leader, you're selling your interpersonal skills. And one of the best skills is getting the other person to talk about himself or herself.

By doing this, you will learn a lot about others and about their roles with the company. You'll find out that Maggie Brey, the manager of customer service, has been with the company for five years, that she likes sky-diving, that she has two small kids, that she collects paperweights....Ding-dong. There's the bell. Next appointment, please.

At last, the introductions and meetings are over and you're going to have to do some real work. You went to school for years, doing all that homework and listening (sort of) to all those teachers, eventually learning all that stuff, and now you're actually going to *use* it. It's like having an open-book test 40 hours every week.

Have this translated into Urdu by midnight

Your boss will probably start you out on one project or one assignment. You might work on it alone or with a team. Be as flexible as you can. An important ground rule: Make sure you understand the assignment before you begin. It wouldn't do to be afraid to clarify what you have to do, then sit at your desk while your boss is on a business trip and realize you don't really know what to do and he wants it done (whatever "it" is) when he returns in two days.

Ask questions. Then, when you think you understand, do this: Repeat what he said (or what you think he said). He'll either agree wholeheartedly, or verbally give you minor changes or corrections. Write down, right then, what is discussed and agreed upon.

Ask for a deadline if he doesn't give you one. Some bosses are vague, "Oh, when you get to it," but that isn't very satisfactory. If he can't be pinned down, take a stab and suggest one of your own (make sure you give yourself enough time; don't go for a quick turn-around to try to impress him). "What about first thing this Thursday morning?" you say. He agrees. Done. Write it down.

If the assignment warrants it, make an appointment with him "first thing" Thursday morning to turn in the assignment. In fact, if he doesn't set up fairly regular times to meet with you, you should initiate this system.

Date books: If it's Tuesday, it must be boss day

A good rule of thumb is to meet with your boss once a week. A little realism has to be brought in here. If he is directly supervising 25 people, this is not going to happen. He may want to meet with you alone less often but meet with your "team" on a weekly basis.

You should arrange some time, even if it's less often than once a week, in which you can sit down with him, just the two of you, and go over your work—discuss current assignments, look ahead at what's coming up and iron out any problems in the work flow.

You will need a very good system for keeping track of meetings, assignment deadlines, follow-up phone calls, etc. If you've never owned a really comprehensive date book before, now is the time to buy one. Check around and find out what your working friends use and like.

Buy one that fits the needs of your job. Your friend may be traveling in a company car and have all kinds of out-of-pocket expenses, and need a place to record them, but if you aren't doing that, you don't want the same kind of date book. You may need one that allows you to record appointments from early in the morning to the evening, another place on the same page for listing deadlines due that day and tasks to be working on, another place for phone calls (names and numbers) to be made that day, etc.

Each morning, you turn over the page to the new day. But be careful: If you had a 7:30 a.m. breakfast meeting with your boss and you turn over the page, promptly at 8 a.m. at your desk, you're dead meat.

Work out an "alert" system. I write down the day before a meeting: "Breakfast Betsy Leary tomorrow 7:30." That reminds me (and I need reminding, as I'm barely conscious at 7:30 a.m.) so that I make sure I show up, at the right place, at the right time.

This is especially important if the meeting is on a Monday morning. To keep from getting an ulcer over the weekend, wondering if you'll forget and knowing that you will, tape a reminder to the bathroom mirror. You'll see it Sunday night, get up in time Monday morning and be at the Horrendous House of Waffles in plenty of time.

I tend to write everything down. But I try to write it down only twice—in two very important places.

First, I write items down in my date book. If I have an assignment due on Tuesday, June 2, then I write it down on the June 2 page, and I also write it down, as a reminder, on the June 1 page (or even earlier, if it's a major assignment).

I also write down tasks that must be done on a particular day. (I agreed in a meeting to call Seattle on Wednesday—the only logical place to write that down is on

Wednesday's page. I don't need to remind myself on Tuesday.)

To do or not to do is *not* in question

I also keep a general "to do" list on the computer. I print it out every day. I keep the printed version on my desk, crossing off items as I complete them and writing in new ones. Every morning, I go into the computer, delete those items I crossed off the day before, add the new ones, and print out the new list. (Each item that has a deadline has that date written beside it.)

The list is always fresh, I don't have scraps of paper here and there all over my desk and I don't forget what I have to do.

Be specific when you write down something you need to do. "Arrange Christmas party for company" just won't do. It's too general and it actually contains about 50 (at least) different tasks. Break big topics down into tasks that you can do and cross off the list. ("Call florist and order 50 centerpieces for $10 each.")

You may have a great memory but don't take false pride in remembering details you don't have to, or ones you might just forget. Keep things written down, in as brief yet understandable form as possible. Otherwise, you'll end up ordering 10 centerpieces for $50 each. (The fact that it's the same amount of money doesn't count.)

But no one told me I couldn't take the computer home. For keeps.

When people are fired, other than for outright dishonesty or because they freaked out and bit the CEO, it's very often for "work habits." Unless, for some strange reason you want to be fired, it's pretty hard to get canned for poor work habits.

When you start the job, you are told: Come to work at 8 a.m., take one hour for lunch, and you're free to go home at 5 p.m. Simple enough. But Princess Julie decides 8:30-ish is good enough, even though there's no one to answer the phones in her area until she gets there. And, well, she once stayed until 5:15 so 90 minutes for lunch is OK, especially with that shoe sale on. And if she doesn't leave at 4:50, she'll never beat the traffic. C'mon, Julie, common sense.

Unless you literally clock in, most people won't know if you are there at 8:00 or 8:05 or 8:15, for that matter, or if you leave a few minutes early, *once in a while*. But a steady habit of coming in late, taking long lunch periods and leaving early (not necessarily all in the same day) creates an atmosphere of ill will (if the other people obey the rules and you don't, they get mad—and they may get even) and it makes you a "time thief."

You are stealing time. Time that you could have—and should have—used to benefit the company. And you are, of course, being paid for work performed between 8 a.m. and lunch, and lunch and 5 p.m. Sure, sometimes, you'll have a headache and need to leave early. Sometimes you have to stop off and leave the cat at the vet. Unless it's truly unexpected, let your boss know you'll be a little late—and then make up the time either that day or, at the latest, that week.

If you believe there should be a constitutional amendment forbidding anyone from unlocking company doors before 9 a.m., you either bite the bullet and do the 8 o'clock shuffle, anyway, or you promote the idea of flex time where you come in at 9 and leave at 6. But you have to play fair. "Flex" doesn't mean coming in at 9 and leaving at 5. And don't try to change the ways of the world as soon as you begin working at a place. Go along with the system. And go to bed earlier.

And once you are at work, work. Most of the time. Not even the CEO is grinding away at his or her desk every minute. You will probably find a pattern in your new office that goes something like this: People arrive at work, get their coats off, go to the bathroom, fix their hair (make-up, ties, etc.), go to the vending machine or cafeteria and get a cup of coffee, and make idle chit-chat for a few minutes (emphasis on "few") before they settle in at their desks. That may be OK, in your corporate culture. It would be a pretty grim world if we walked silently into the building, heads down, went to our desks and began to work. A little chatting about current events, the weather, soap operas, sports is all right.

Remember the relative leisure of those mornings on the days when you have to make your way through snow drifts to be at a 7 a.m. meeting with 30 other people (where you are helping your unpopular boss make a presentation on a controversial topic) and the coffee machine is broken. Those days happen, too.

In addition to giving a full day's work for a full day's pay, be careful of too much chit-chat during the day, either with other employees or on the phone. This work habit may be a little harder to control since other people are involved, people you don't always have control over.

This job is cutting into my personal time!

You can control your personal time on the phone. When the times are extraordinary, you may have to make arrangements: I remember going to my boss when I was closing on the sale of a house and asking her indulgence while I made and received *a lot* of calls from brokers, real-estate agents, bankers, plumbers, *ad mortgageam*. She was understanding—and appreciated the fact that I made up the time later.

On a typical day, you should keep your personal calls to a couple quick ones to family or friends. It's very bad form for your boss to come by your office and find you on the phone *again* obviously discussing something personal. Even if you say, when she walks up, "Gotta go. I'll call you later," and you turn your attention to her, it still makes a negative impression. (*Especially* if that report is overdue and you claimed you just "couldn't get it done any sooner.")

If the problem is the person calling you—your boyfriend doesn't seem to understand that you've forsaken campus life for a real job—you'll have to tell him, flat out, that you just can't talk to him more than once a day and for only five minutes at a time. Or meet him for lunch from time to time (keeping it to one hour, of course) and stay off the phone with him altogether.

Time theft and other office crimes

There are other kinds of theft in addition to "time theft" that we may not think of as stealing. Some people feel the company photocopier is there for them to reproduce anything and everything in their personal lives from yard-sale fliers to ads for some homemade jewelry they're selling out of their bottom drawer (on company time, of course).

Some employees who have access to company postage stamps will even use them for their own letters. Or they'll make long-distance calls to family and friends from their desks. (If you must call someone during working hours, use your phone-company calling card and charge it to your home phone.)

Stealing of this nature and degree usually won't get you arrested, or even fired, but it will reflect poorly on you and can cause your supervisors to question your honesty, your judgment and your common sense. At worst, you might receive a reprimand (how would you like your personnel file to carry the information that you "used company postage for personal use"), be made to reimburse the company and have one heck of a time getting promotions or commendations later. Don't risk it.

Few employers would object if an employee didn't own a personal computer and stayed after work to write personal letters on the one at his desk. Unlike the postage, though, this isn't really "using" anything (the employee is printing out on his own personal letterhead) and it's being done on the employee's own time, albeit at the employer's office.

So what's wrong with a little (OK, a lot) of cleavage?

You knew how people tended to dress in your office before you ever took the job. If you decide, after a period of time, that you don't want to dress as is expected of you, you could cause trouble for yourself. Some companies try to combat this feeling by creating occasional "casual days," where everyone is allowed to dress down (within reason).

But if you are dressing too casually all of the time, expect your supervisor to discuss this with you. You may not agree philosophically with the fact that you are expected to wear skirts and not slacks, or that you must wear suits and not sports coats *every day*, but you didn't walk into this job blindfolded, I'm sure.

Your workspace: A corner cubicle with a view

It's unlikely that you'll have a private office. The trend for many years has been to get rid of walls and use moveable cubicles. Even your boss may have a similar arrangement, only bigger. Each cubicle has drawers, shelving, a small bulletin board, a computer set-up, but probably not a free-standing desk. Count yourself lucky if you have a window.

Also count yourself lucky if you are not working near people who are loud. The disadvantage of open cubicles is that noise will carry, even with the acoustical padding on all the walls. If the person two or three cubicles down from you is a loud talker, it will drive you to distraction until you learn to tune him or her out and get on with your work.

Of course, with the cubicle arrangement, you won't be able to get that after-lunch nap you cherished so much in college. There isn't much privacy: Anyone walking by can see right into your area and observe you making a paper-clip airplane while talking on the phone to your girlfriend.

And now, gentle reader, a word from Miss Manners

Office etiquette also requires a goodly dose of common sense. For example, how do you address your boss? Your *boss's* boss? The CEO? Visitors? It's better to use the "Mr." and "Ms." approach and let them urge you to use a first name than get too casual too soon and be informed that they are "*Mr.* Smith."

We Americans run a pretty egalitarian society, but you still don't want to get too first-name-ish with people far above you in rank at the company. Even if your boss, who may be several years older than you and have a few years' seniority at the company, calls his boss, "Jake," you will want to start out with "Mr. Herbert." Let *Jake* insist on being called Jake.

You don't have to be so sickeningly polite that you make everyone deathly ill, but observing good rules of behavior will never go out of style (these rules apply equally to both genders):

- If you are entering a senior person's office for the first time, remain standing until he or she asks you to sit down.
- Don't put your coffee cup on his or her nice desk or table without first asking for a coaster.

- Offer to get more chairs—and then do it—when a lot of people come into a room for a meeting.
- Never be too loud.
- Don't interrupt when other people are talking.
- Never tell jokes that offend any group. Just because the person listening to the joke is a white male doesn't mean he thinks jokes ridiculing women are funny.
- Don't be late to meetings. It's rude to everyone else who must waste their precious time while waiting for you.
- Don't interrupt your boss and co-workers when they're on the phone, or talking with others. It doesn't make it OK because you ask, "May I interrupt?" first.
- If you're meeting with someone in your workspace, don't take a phone call and have a lengthy conversation. Either end the phone call as quickly as possible, or postpone your discussion.
- Return phone calls and respond to requests for information as soon as possible, whether it's an outside client, your boss or your co-worker.

Well, you get the picture. Look back at this list. Is there anything here (and you know that this is the tip of the social iceberg) that's not common sense?

There is something known as business etiquette, as well. It's translating social etiquette into a business setting.

Thank you so much for smiling at me in the hall this a.m.

For example, do not fail to write thank-you notes or memos or letters to people who have been helpful in one way or another, as long as you don't overdo it. Not every single act of simple human kindness needs to have a written acknowledgment; in fact, people who continually crank these things out also turn other people deathly ill (they are very often the same people who make smiling faces as the dots above i's).

As a new, low-level employee, you won't have a lot of occasions to send such a memo or letter, but keep this in mind: When someone in the company has been very helpful, you are doing a service by writing a short memo, specifying what he or she did that was appreciated ("Your efficient handling of the Spitzer account made it possible for our team to close the deal in record time.") and send a copy of the memo to the person's boss (who should, in turn, forward it to the person's personnel file).

Meetings

If you are required to attend meetings, sometimes on behalf of your boss, arrive on time, don't talk too long (if at all—sometimes new people are expected to shut up and take notes), bring the items your boss told you to bring, have enough copies for everyone, make sure the charts are printed neatly and big enough for everyone to see, concentrate on making your boss look good, and, if you are supposed to do any follow-up, do it.

A quick course in corporate psychology

A new employee is required to be an amateur psychologist (and sometimes you wonder if you aren't being asked to be a *professional* one). One of the areas in which you will more than earn your B.A. in Psychology will be in the studying, analyzing and reacting to management styles (a manifestation of personality traits).

Let's look at a few of these types of managers. No doubt, your first boss will have some of these characteristics:

Charlie the undecided

Charlie does everything by consensus. He seems incapable of making a decision without the group discussing it, dissecting it and then coming, slowly, to a conclusion. He believes it's democracy in action, but Charlie never learned that a manager is not a democrat (*small* d, that is); he is a benevolent dictator. As a result, work performed by his unit may have the blessing of everyone in it. But other managers are being overworked because no one wants to go to Charlie's group any more as it takes *too long to get results.*

Charlie wants to be liked. He doesn't understand that sometimes making wise, but hard decisions would be appreciated by his staff instead of deliberating for hours over the same topic. When tough decisions have to be made, many bosses say to themselves, with a sigh, "Well, that's what I'm getting paid for." In fact, a lot of managers are fired or demoted because they are unable or unwilling to make a decision. And sometimes making *any* decision is preferable to not making one at all and keeping a whole department or a whole company sitting on its hands.

One of the characteristics of higher and higher salaries and bigger and bigger titles is the increased responsibility that goes with it. Most vice presidents have to make decisions that affect the hiring and firing of the people. (Since the only command you'll be giving in your first job will be to say, "I'll take fries with that," to the cook in the cafeteria, you have a while to wait before you make the Big Ones.)

Janet the unkind

Janet is a dictator, though "benevolent" would not be a word often used in the same sentence as her name. "I want it and I want it *now*!" she has been heard to say on the phone to one of her subordinates at least once in a while (OK, twice a day). She has little use for people who decide things on an emotional basis. What's the bottom line? Will it profit her division? The company? Can she get it *now*?

People who are drivers are going to push, push, push and demand work from you that you cannot always provide. They are good for you in that they are demanding, making you demand a lot of yourself, if you don't drop from exhaustion. Sometimes a driver can work for another driver and they get along famously, both pushing themselves to the brink. Other times, they are so much alike they practically recoil when they pass one another in the hallway.

Herb the excited

Herb is a congenial fellow. He's a little loud, a little too quick to act before thinking, but he keeps the meetings moving and the juices flowing. Sometimes (about once every 35 minutes) someone who works for him will hang up the phone and say, with astonishment, "Did you hear what he just promised the Acme Company?" It's exciting to work for him, but it's a bit like trying to keep the streets spotless while following a parade of elephants—and all they gave you was a teaspoon.

Herb does make decisions. They are often wrong, but they do keep the action moving. When creating and testing new campaigns for products or services, sometimes he has to make a lot of decisions and see which ones work. That's why they throw money—sometimes a lot of money—into "research and development."

Diane the rewrite woman

Diane wonders why all the people who work for her are stupid. Of course, she has never said such a thing; in fact, she gets along with most of the people most of the time. But they know from her comments and her actions that she does not approve of what they are doing. Ever.

Not a memo can be sent out without her reviewing it. Unfortunately, she travels a lot so she doesn't always return the memos right away. A lot of her work is done on airplanes where she writes, in red, along the margins of a report or a memo, "This is sophomoric!" She doesn't just review. She rewrites. Hardly a sentence is left alone. And, when you send back *her* words to her, she rewrites *them*.

Not surprisingly, creativity in her department is at a standstill, further "proving" that her people cannot do the work that she has to do for them.

Other managers look for strengths in their people. She looks for weaknesses. And—surprise—she finds them.

She is a "control freak." Diane doesn't understand that power comes from sharing, not from hoarding it.

These are pretty one-dimensional drawings of managers, but they are intended to show you some of the characteristics of people and the management styles that their own personalities dictate.

All of your jobs are intense learning experiences. This is especially true of your first job. You don't have to work for someone who is a certified basket case (although some of us can remember doing so), but use the experience as a great laboratory where you, the subject, are being paid for the experience.

We learn by negative example as often, if not more so, than we learn by positive ones. You may not find a lot of role models at your first job, but you will find people to learn from. Any of the managers described in this chapter will teach you a great deal, although they often will be teaching you what *not* to do. If you find yourself saying, "When I'm a boss, I won't do that," the teaching is taking hold.

And no boss is all bad. You may have to search pretty hard sometimes for the positive characteristics, but they're there. Charlie, for example, will listen to your ideas and give you the chance to fail. And, if you fail, he will help you learn why you failed so that you won't do it again.

Janet will teach you the value of deadlines. Her methods in getting the work done on time may border on the crude, but she does turn in good work in good time. Take her dedication to deadlines and some of Charlie's personable approach and begin to build your own "boss persona."

Herb will listen (but not for too long, so make it brief and to the point) and then he'll agree to let you try something that other managers would say ahead of time was doomed to fail. He gives you that buzz that entrepreneurs feel when they have taken on a big task that they know can succeed if only people will believe in them—and lend them enough money. Herb, by his impatience with explanations, trains you to reduce your comments to a concise, easy-to-digest size, instead of letting you drone on and on...

And Diane? Diane trains you to work hard on dusting off your resume and reading the want ads once again. Seriously, because she has such a fixation with how things should be written, she drives you to express yourself in other ways and broaden your approach to many tasks.

It may not be fair, but they were here first

It's important for you to adapt *your* working style to the working style of your boss and not expect your boss to adapt to you, even if she would or could.

Everything you learn from one manager, you take with you to the next one. You soon earn that equivalent of a B.A. in Psychology—or at least a name tag that says "Lab Rat."

Chapter Eight

Your First Job: 90 Days and Counting

Settling Into a Routine... Sort of

Your first 90 days on the job is called a "probationary period." No, it doesn't mean that you can get wild on Day 91 and tell everyone what you really think of them. It just means that you have passed muster. Now, everyone can rest easier and believe that they made the right choice in hiring you and you can agree with them.

By the end of the 90-day period, you will be fully covered by insurance, you can find your way to the rest room and back and you know to avoid the cafeteria's Hungarian goulash with its "12 secret ingredients" (none of which is apparently a food item).

Your first review

You will probably receive at least an oral review, if not a written one, at the end of your 90 days. We'll talk more about performance reviews in the next chapter, but just a couple of notes here: Reviews shouldn't contain any great surprises. You shouldn't be under the impression that your boss thinks you're doing a great job and then you find out that he has rated you with 4s and 5s (when 1s are tops) on almost everything. Bad boss.

A review, when done well, can be a very educational experience. It gives both you and your boss the opportunity to discuss your performance and how you fit in with the department and the company.

To avoid a rude surprise at 90 days (such as, "We've decided to terminate your employment...") or even a less-than-best review, listen hard for comments from your boss and from others during your first weeks on the job.

Is your boss critical of certain things you have done? Are there misunderstandings? If so, you absolutely must get them cleared up right away.

A misunderstanding is like the fuzzy stuff on that food at the back of your fridge. If you don't do something about it, it won't go away, it will just get bigger.

Just hope that your boss knows your name by now

If your boss isn't good about giving you feedback, learn to ask for it. I don't mean that you should try to get him to praise you. I mean that you should seek to get an honest appraisal of how you are doing. Specific feedback is the best kind. Even positive comments, if too general, aren't all that helpful. "You're doing a great job" is certainly nice to hear but you should find out why he thinks so.

Is it because you meet deadlines? Is it because you are able to gather a lot of information and compile it into one, concise report? Is it because you, through your hard work and warm personality, are building bridges with other departments and with suppliers or customers?

Conversely, where do you need improvement? No one is going to give you a detailed run-down after 90 days, but you will have had enough time to show your stuff—or *not* show it.

Your good performance has a domino effect. If you demonstrate superior performance to your boss, he will bring your performance to the attention of his boss, and his boss's boss—and others. Remember what I said earlier: Make your boss look good. You may have a boss who steals all the credit for everything you do, and such disgusting people do exist, but most bosses will give you credit or, at worst, share it.

When he shares the credit, but not the salary

"This report is excellent," says your boss's boss to your boss. "Who did it?" If he mentions your name, place one gold star on your bulletin board. If he takes credit for it, it may not be all bad, even if it does border on the slightly unethical. By making your boss look good in the eyes of *his* boss, you are winning brownie points with him. Besides, his boss may not believe he did the work. She may have seen your boss's report writing and know that he couldn't put such good work together if he had a year. She'll eventually find out who you are.

Don't make the mistake of trying to please or impress someone at a level higher than your boss, bypassing him in the process. Bad employee.

I'd give you your review now, but we're due at the ball park

You may think you'll be good buddies with your boss, especially if he's not much older than you are, but don't expect this to happen. It would be awkward for him, in fact, to get too chummy and then have to turn around and deal with you as a subordinate. It doesn't mean you can't go to lunch together now and then or sit around after hours and argue about the Mets, but don't push it.

A good working relationship with your boss, based on mutual respect, with a feeling that each is a "really nice person," certainly makes for a pleasant working environment, helps you get your work done—and helps your performance rating. Here's hoping you'll have such a relationship with every job you ever have. In spite of the negative portrayals of some boss "types" in the previous chapter, you will find that most bosses are reasonable people most of the time.

Whatever situation you find yourself in, try hard to have a good working relationship. Life's too short to have anything else.

Office gossip: I've got their number —and they've got mine

By this time, you probably have a very good idea of the strengths and weaknesses of your fellow employees. You know who keeps promises to get you information on time, who can't ever seem to concentrate on the task at hand, who is on time, who has her eye on the boss's job...

You also know a lot of personal information about most of the people you work with, sometimes more information than you really care to know, and they know some about you.

Which brings up the juicy side of corporate life: office gossip. You can be assured that every personal item you share with certain co-workers will end up being shared within 30 minutes with every available person within 30 cubicles. (It's what I call the "30/30 Rule.")

If one of your co-workers tells you everything you want to know—and *don't* want to know—about everyone else in the office, take a tip from me: That should be a Big Clue not to tell this person anything you don't want spread over the company and beyond.

"Kill the messenger" may not be a bad idea

Every company has a handful of Messengers of Gossip (MOGs). Whether the gossip is true, recent or relevant is irrelevant. It's an item that must be shared with inquiring and non-inquiring minds alike.

Typical scene: MOG Tom comes flying into your cubicle on a dark Monday morning. Breathlessly, he says, "Did you hear about Molly?" You can't tell from his performance if Molly died or got promoted. Of course, you have to respond: "No, what?"

"She's pregnant!"

You may be quite excited about this or you may not really care. You may barely know Molly. But that doesn't stop a certified MOG.

If you wish to avoid more details, you're going to have to grab a folder, stand up rapidly and flat-out lie. "Love to stay and talk, but I've got a meeting," then flee for five minutes to somewhere else.

MOG Tom won't mind. Before you can exit your cubicle, he's in someone else's face, saying, with equal breathless enthusiasm: "Did you hear about Molly?"

Poor Molly. It may not even be true. And even if it is, she probably didn't want freelance publicist Tom to fly through the building, tossing her name—and motherhood status—everywhere.

You might only have to say to the MOG, "Boy, do I have a headache" and it can be translated into rumors of brain tumors ("You know, it does seem that he hasn't looked well lately and—he did have that doctor's appointment about a month ago") or hangovers ("You should have seen him at Anne's party last week!").

Being provided with tidbits of gossip is one thing. Sharing them with others is another. Again, the information may not be true, it may be—and often is—none of your business, and it can cause great ill will within a department or company if you persist in it. Instead, concentrate on gossiping about Britain's Royal Family or the latest scandal in Washington.

Working with different work styles

Just as you need to recognize the various personalities and working styles of your supervisor, you also need to understand the working styles of your co-workers in order to avoid a negative impact on your own performance.

Let's say that you have to pass on a report to Lois before it can be given to your boss. You discover that Lois is a good worker but she is very methodical and she will not put your work ahead of what is already on her desk. Unlike the other people who have to review and comment on the report who return it to you in two days, Lois will take at least five.

Work with her. She won't change. She might change, a little, for *her* supervisor but you're on her level so you're out of luck. Build extra time into the reporting time frame, giving her five days. This way, she handles it on her own terms, gives you a good response and you don't get an ulcer.

When you do come across what you perceive as shortcomings in your co-workers (don't worry, they'll find them in you, too), see how you can work with them or, at worst, around them.

Oh, was that meeting scheduled for *this* morning?

Your boss wants your five-member team to meet twice a week. If it is convenient for four out of five of you to get together early in the morning, maybe over coffee in the cafeteria, but the fifth person, Larry, who is needed at the meeting, never shows up on time, or never even shows up at all, because of—count 'em—50 different excuses, maybe an 8 a.m. meeting just won't work. Try another time.

You don't have to make compromises for everyone. Nobody is asking you to be a doormat or a martyr. But think of it this way: What can you and others do to insure that the work is done well and on time? If it means pushing and pulling a little here and there to make room for people's idiosyncrasies, work habits, traumas, etc., so be it.

Too often, we get bogged down by the fact that we "can't" meet at 8 a.m. because Larry has all those family obligations and....Work around it.

Or we "can't" get the reports in on time because Lois is so rigid she won't push your request to the top of the pile...Work around it.

Everyone loves a facilitator. If you develop this skill you will win the hearts (and high performance ratings) of the others, including your boss who will continue hearing good things about you.

"I don't know how she does it, but she can even get along with Bonnie!" someone will exclaim about you. It's not that hard, really. You just have to have a lot of patience, tolerance for various ways of doing things and a steely eyed, focused determination to make something work whether it's because of or in spite of certain other people.

Volunteering for other assignments

Reflect, frequently, on your role in the organization and how you can enhance what should already be a positive image. Volunteering for assignments is an excellent way to impress your boss. It may also give you options you wouldn't have if the assignments are just handed out.

Volunteering for other tasks *outside* the department is also important. With your boss's permission, you can help organize the blood drive or the company's annual picnic. It's a way to get you out of your cubicle and into view of people from other departments. (Always think ahead. "I may be working for one of these people within the next 12 months," is a thought that should cross your mind just about every time you walk into a room of people from different departments.)

If there is a department that sounds exciting, learn what you can about it. Read up on it, follow its news in the company newsletter, get to know some of the people at or near your level in the area. Then, when an opening does occur, you will not be starting out cold.

Help other people. If they are floundering under assignments that are overwhelming them, give them some assistance. They'll help you, in turn, when you need it.

If you are part of a team, act like it. Your accomplishments will stand out on an individual basis, but be a team player and make an effort to pull together to finish the work.

When your boss compliments you, be gracious and thank her, but turn it around, too. "I really enjoy working here. I'm pleased to be working for you. You've really given me a chance to get in there and find out what this department is all about." Don't consider this fawning behaviour. You, simply and honestly, are expressing that you appreciate the opportunity to work in an area you enjoy. Gold stars all around!

If you are impressed by how someone conducts herself in front of a group or writes so clearly and concisely or seems to handle contradictory needs in an effortless manner, learn how she does it. Talk to her. Tell her what you've observed and ask for her advice. She will, of course, be flattered and she'll be impressed that you are so sincere about it.

Office romance: Finally we're getting to the good stuff!

Now, let's talk about kissing and hugging.

Oooooh, you're thinking, I wondered when he'd get to that part.

Kissing and hugging is good. But not when it's between people in the same department or division. Or, sometimes, even in the same company.

When romantic involvement occurs between co-workers, or especially between supervisor and supervised, it can spell trouble. Dating someone colors your judgment. Your company won't like it if you are dating someone you have to work with and you are expected to review his or her work (or vice versa).

If the two of you work on the same level, but are part of a small team, it can be difficult for both of you and for your fellow team members. Every comment either of you makes can be taken out of context; any disagreement between you can be interpreted as coming from or spilling over into your after-hours life. Whether it's true, the others in the room are uncomfortable with your "mixing" work with your personal lives.

Even if you work together only occasionally, the same semi-awkward situation persists. Everyone in the room is aware that you are dating and they make assumptions about what you say that may or may not be true.

And, frankly, it can wreak havoc with your personal relationship, too. ("What did you mean today," he says, "when you criticized my report?" She, in turn, raises her eyebrows, "Mean? I meant just what I said: It needs work." This conversation should not be carried on while one or the other is slicing vegetables with a very sharp knife.)

To avoid such situations developing, look for romantic interest elsewhere. If Cupid is determined, however, that you're going to fall head over heels in love with Melissa in

Accounting ("She's got these beautiful eyes that sparkle when she's processing purchase orders"), the two of you need to make sure you are not headed for disaster. If you don't work directly together, it may be OK. If you do work together or you are about to, take drastic measures: See if one of you can't get transferred to another, neutral area.

Some companies don't forbid dating but they do forbid spouses to work for the same company. Be prepared for one of you to leave the company if wedding bells loom.

The real danger comes about when a person is dating someone for whom he or she works. Bad, bad, bad. No one is going to win on this one. The boss is throwing herself into a bad situation; the subordinate is doing the same; everyone else working for and with them has a right to be very concerned about how this affects their relationship with both people, especially with the boss.

This, too, is often forbidden in many companies. Transfers out of the department or new jobs elsewhere can, of course, take care of the situation—and should, ASAP.

What about friendships? Go for it. You will make some wonderful friends at your first job. Just one word of warning: If you socialize with work friends exclusively, you'll end up spending a lot of time talking about work and when you do go back to the office on Monday it won't seem like you've been gone. Develop a good selection of work friends and nonwork friends and mix them together.

Peace and quiet, that's what I want

If you asked your boss "What do you want from your employees?" What would he or she say? What does a boss want from you? Let's make a list:

1. Make *his or her* boss think he's doing a good job.
2. Get the work done well.
3. Get it done on time or ahead of time.

4. Save the company (department, team) money.
5. Be polite and personable: Get along with everyone.
6. Be honest.
7. Work hard.
8. Work smart.
9. Have good work habits.
10. Look good.
11. Make a good impression on visitors, vendors, clients, the general public.
12. Be skilled at whatever talents the department needs (accounting practices, writing articles, sales techniques).

That's all. Look, you had these attributes before you started working here. You didn't suddenly develop honesty or a friendly attitude toward other people. You have, by the 90th day or the sixth month, learned a lot of things on the job, about the industry, the company, what your department does, what it needs to do—but the rest of this list is stuff you brought with you.

Let's see, five pencils at a nickel each...

Let's look for a minute at a couple of these. Number 4 says you should save money. Just because you share a $100,000 budget doesn't mean you have to spend it all. Look for creative, common-sense approaches to reducing costs. Nothing makes a boss (and other bosses, all the way up to the CEO) perk up more than if you can say you can handle something for $6,000 when it used to cost $12,000. Keep your eye out for money-saving ways to do things, once you begin to understand how the system works.

Number 11 bears looking at too. Remember that, when you attend a seminar or go to a business lunch, you are representing the corporation. Something dumb by you is repeated as, "Anna Smith from Clements Industries said..." not just "Anna Smith said..."

An error first-jobbers sometimes make is trying too hard. If a visitor asks you something about the company and you don't know, just say so. If it's important enough, or the visitor is important enough, jot it down, find out and let him or her know later. That will impress them. Don't fudge an answer or take a wild stab. As sure as you do, when the visitor is safely delivered by you to the CEO herself, you will hear, "This young man just told me you..." If you, "the young man," took a wild guess, you'll not be able to get the burn marks off your suit where the CEO's angry eyes bore through you. And, by no coincidence, you may be called into your boss's office that same day and be told to take a refresher course in company history.

Are those deadlines in your face?

You know what "work hard" means, but how about "work smart"? You work smart so you don't have to work so hard. Joe and Jane both have reports due to their boss by Friday at 5 p.m. Jane knows that Lois will demand more time to get her part of the report ready, so she builds in more time. Joe either knows it and ignores it or he hasn't learned from his experience. At any rate, he gives his request to Lois two days later than he should have.

Similar choices are made by Joe and Jane down the line, resulting in Jane's report being completed and in on time and Joe begging an extension until Monday morning.

Jane worked smart. She sat down when she first got the assignment and decided how she was going to get the work done on time. She succeeded. Joe, on the other hand, figured that, since he could write reports blindfolded—and he can—he was in no major danger. He didn't figure on Fred being on vacation this week, on Lois' recalcitrance, on accounting being too busy with end-of-the-year reports to give him the time he needed...

You can't anticipate everything, but you need to sit back and view the whole situation. Give time to the details and to the whole picture. What has to be done and who has to do it to make it work? Jane spent less time on the report than Joe did, and hers is in a binder sitting on the boss's desk. Because he became preoccupied with this report, he's already behind on another project the boss gave him to do. And Lois needs to provide some information to him. Do you think he'll approach her differently this time? Work smart.

So, How'm I doing?

Evaluate your own performance, based on this list and on other attributes your boss is concerned about. How are you doing? Go to human resources and ask for a copy of the evaluation form that will be used in your performance reviews. (The first will probably occur at the end of your first six months). See what your boss will be filling out. Honestly now, how are you doing in each of these areas? Rate yourself, trying not to be too critical or too forgiving. Where has the boss been critical or, at least, not praising? Where has he said you were really doing a good job?

If you are at the end of your first 90 days, you are halfway through the first six months and 90 days away from the first formal (i.e., write it down and put it in your personnel file) review.

Make a pact with yourself. Build the areas where you are weakest and continue to perform well in the areas where you already are being recognized. Make the 180th day your finish line. Run!

Self-evaluation never ends. After years of successfully performing in the corporate world, you will still need to review your own performance from time to time, ahead of your boss, so that you can identify weak areas and work on strengthening them before you are told to do so. Planned self-improvement is such a rare virtue that, when we embark upon it and successfully reach our goals, we astound everyone.

Planes, trains, automobiles and expense reports

In your first job, you aren't likely to travel much for the company, unless you're a salesperson on the road, but I'll give you a few tips:

1. Keep your receipts. Companies aren't likely to reimburse you for out-of-pocket expenses if you can't provide receipts. And keep good, overall records of all financial details for the whole trip. It's not that they don't trust you (although they might not); it's because they, in turn, may have to provide the receipts to the IRS.

   It's a good idea to pay for everything you can with a charge card so that you have a written, traceable record. You'll still have to turn in receipts, but you'll have a back-up.

   Certain expenses, such as tipping, should be covered by the company without requiring receipts, but such items are few.
2. Obtain the company policies on business travel and read them carefully. It can be costly for you if you don't! Suppose you attend a convention where breakfast on Tuesday is covered by the registration fee, but you decide to have breakfast at the hotel before you walk across the street. Accounting could decide that you will have to pay for that meal yourself since the company had already paid for the one you didn't eat. A few of

those bloopers and suddenly you've got a *personal* tab of $100.

3. Don't get wild. You're young and single and you've never been to New Orleans before. You can have a lot of fun, by anybody's standards, but you're there to represent your corporation and not your drinking group at college. Just be careful.
4. Have all important trip-related information written down on your computer and carry a printed copy with you. It will include hotel name, address, phone, fax and your confirmation number; flight numbers and arrival and departure times; contact people names, addresses, phones, faxes, appointment times and places.

   Should you lose this paper, call back to your office and have someone fax another copy to you. Keeping this information in one handy place isn't something that only first-timers do; this is something all smart corporate travelers do.
5. Don't let the post-travel work overwhelm you once you get back in the office. Try to leave behind on your desk only a reasonable amount of work before you go, instead of stacks and stacks, and take some (but only "some") work with you to handle on the trip. You can get a lot of work done in airports, hotel lobbies and on airplanes—and you won't have to face doing it all upon your return.

   And it still leaves you time to enjoy Paris (or Peoria).

Chapter Nine

Your Annual Review (Has It Been a Year Already?)

Retirement In 42 Years!

By the end of the first year, you'll know whether you like working for this company, whether you like working for this boss, whether you like working, *period*.

You've come a long way since that first 90-day review. You've had a chance to do some actual work, as well as learn a lot along the way, make some new friends and get to know the corporate culture.

You've also given your boss the chance to see how quickly and how well you learn, how you perform certain tasks, how you take criticism, how you interact with other employees and with her, even how well-prepared you might be to move up the ladder.

Fancy meeting you here

Although you're not ready for senior management yet and that fabled key to the executive washroom (which is usually left unlocked, so you really don't need the key), you should have begun to show your boss and others what kind of potential you have.

Since this was your first year on the job, you probably had a review after the first 90 days and a more formal review after the first six months. Now, it's time for the long awaited annual review—to which salary increases are most often contingent upon.

As with any previous reviews you've had, you should be well-prepared for your annual review. You may be asked to evaluate yourself, prepare questions you may have or issues you'd like to discuss. You may even be asked to evaluate your boss of the department at this time.

And, as I've said before, if you've had good ongoing communication with your boss, very little of what occurs at your review should come as a surprise. If there *were* any problems with your performance, you should have worked to improve by now.

Performance reviews in general are positive, learning experiences. It gives both you and your boss the opportunity to discuss your past performance and look ahead at what you expect to accomplish in the next 6 or 12 months.

Sticks and stones—and bad reviews —may break my bones

But, let's look at a negative situation—and how you can learn from it and work to prevent it next time.

Suppose your boss tossed a real zinger at you. He criticized you for something you felt was unfair, thus marking you down in one category (or more), perhaps even causing you not to get a raise or bonus that was tied to a higher evaluation.

First of all, remain calm. Don't go on the attack. Let him say what he has to say, listen intently, and then ask questions. Don't go on the defensive. Not immediately, that is. The question-asking time is to give you a chance to work through what he has to say and to find out, in more detail, what he is talking about.

Let's say he is criticizing you for your work habits. He says you "often come to work late."

Those are rather vague charges. You have the right to have his criticism spelled out a little more clearly than that.

He may have detailed records, which indicate several lates under your name. Or he may just have remembered the time he was looking for you at 8:05 a.m. and you weren't at your desk. We should be able to assume that he has spoken to you about this already if he is going to write it down on your evaluation. But not all bosses play fair. He may have, semi-innocently, assumed that you "knew" he was upset because you knew you were supposed to be seated by 8 a.m. five days a week.

But, even without supporting, written evidence, suppose that you feel your boss's criticism in your review is patently unfair. He might have come by your desk or called you on the phone on one of the *few* mornings you have been late. He may have decided that you were "always" late since you weren't there then. The fact that he never knew for sure, one way or the other, on any other morning isn't something he considers necessary to check out.

Try to pin him down on his criticism. If he refers to this one morning (and you may not even know this "incident" occurred if he didn't say anything at the time), you have the right to point out that you are "rarely" late and that you often stay late to work on a report, attend a meeting, take care of some long-distance calls to other time zones, etc.

Yesterday, you took 65 minutes for lunch! So there!

It's important that you handle this discussion in a professional manner. After all, it *is* your boss you're talking to. And, whatever the final outcome, you *will* have to continue to work together—you hope. He may be an unfair (expletive deleted), but he is holding a lot of the cards in his hands. Don't blow it by getting angry, by getting accusatory, by saying things like, "Well, *you* don't always get here on time! I came by your office just this morning and you weren't here yet at 9 a.m.!"

This sort of shoving match will earn you no points; and, with your luck, you'll find out he was upstairs consoling another employee who just found out a relative had died.

Keep the discussion civil and polite. "As you know, I'm also often here after hours to complete work or handle anything that has come up," you can say. The "as you know" is thrown in there because you know he knows it. You often are meeting with him at that time or he sees you there.

A fairly brief, civil discussion is called for. Make your point, be as specific as possible, be as open and friendly as possible. If you still think he is basing the criticism on one occasion, ask him, "Are there other times that you are thinking of when I was late?" Unless he can push the sign-in register across the desk at you showing you proof, he probably will have to say no.

You might be able to get him to rewrite the criticism and give you a higher evaluation. In most companies, the subordinate must be given the opportunity to be reviewed, read the written evaluation and respond to it, verbally and in writing, before it is passed on to human resources (to put a copy in your personnel file) and to your boss's boss.

So, I'm not perfect

If he admits he made a mistake (we're on rather treacherous ground here), he may agree to amend the rating and the written criticism.

If he won't do that, at least you have the opportunity to provide a written rebuttal to his comments. Think hard about what you will say, if you decide to do that. When you're up for another job at this company in 18 months, and the person you are seeking to work for gets your personnel file and reads your rebuttal, what will he or she think?

If the rebuttal has an angry, defensive tone, it will give the reader pause: "Do I really want to hire this person?" Others won't know if you were late or not. They may not even know your present boss (he may be gone from the company already) or, if they do, they don't know what kind of a boss he is. They only know him as a fellow manager, not as a boss. And they probably don't know you.

Calm down!! Calm down!!

Write and rewrite your rebuttal several times. See how it looks (literally) beside the boss' comments. Keep the *tone* reasonable and polite. "Mr. Patton's comments appear to be based on one incident in a six-month period. I was at work on time on other occasions and, in fact, often stayed after hours to complete tasks and handle emergencies."

If you write a reasonable rebuttal, you are demonstrating to anyone who reads your file that you have guts enough to stand up for yourself but you aren't wild-eyed and crazed by what is really a fairly mild criticism.

Use the review process as a learning exercise. First, learn what upsets your boss. If he is a stickler for people being at work at 8 a.m., you've got a screw loose if you expect to wander in later than that and keep him happy. OK, so you stay late, so you work really smart, so you never fail to meet a deadline. He has a fixation on people being there "on time." Live with it.

If you're under your desk, make a noise

Learn to watch for signals. Did he say to you, in passing, "I came by your desk at 8:15 this morning and I missed you." Hey, if you were in the building and were already in a meeting—or even if you were getting a cup of coffee—make darned sure he knows that. Right then. But take his comment as a warning.

If he tends to come by your desk between 8:00 and 8:15 (he may be doing this to everyone to make sure they're at work), plan your coffee-hunting for another time. And, if you are in a meeting, put a sign on your desk that says, "7:45 a.m. In meeting in Accounting on Budget. Return at 9:00."

How to handle a boss with Review-*phobia*

Sometimes, bosses avoid giving reviews because they hate the intense one-on-one discussions, no matter how pleasant, that are a part of the process. If you work for such a boss, you may wait weeks, even months, for your review. Human resources will probably have sent a reminder notice to your boss, telling him which employees' reviews are due by which dates. The boss keeps intending to do it, but, since he hates it, he keeps putting it off. In the meantime, you are getting more and more anxious.

You will simply have to bite the bullet and talk with your boss. You'll have to remind him when the review was due. If you're smart, you'll have your calendar with you and ask for an appointment for the review right then. If the boss later cancels the appointment, you'll have to repeat the process.

Since a salary review is usually attached to the performance review, this is more than just talking about work habits and interpersonal relationships. At least, a late review means that the salary increase, if there is one, will be retroactive to the original review date, but most of us would still rather see the review (and the increase) take place when it's scheduled.

If you simply can't budge your boss, more drastic steps may have to be taken. Go talk with a friend in human resources. (If you haven't made friends with anyone in this department, you can sure be labeled "risk-taker.") Explain the situation and enlist his or her help. Perhaps it can result in a stronger memo to your boss from a manager in human resources to get him to act. If he is late with your review, he's probably late with everyone else's. If each of you seeks to get him to act, to no avail, then individual complaints to human resources may bring results.

Don't forget those friendly people in HR

Let's step back in time for a moment: In your first few months on the job, you will want to learn the details (actual policies, as well as how things are "probably" going to occur) of promotions, transfers, salary increases and other topics, because they'll mean a great deal to you later.

The human resources office is your best source for this information. They are the guardians of the policies and they can take you through the steps. If you attempt to discuss this with your boss, he may give you wrong information because he doesn't want to admit he doesn't understand it all, or he may wonder why you are so interested in promotions and transfers when you've been with the company only three months.

Paranoid bosses may even think you are eyeballing their jobs or you are seeking to jump ship and work in another department. It could cause problems for you even though, logically, it shouldn't. Go to human resources.

Bob Cratchit wants *another* raise only six years later?

Now, we're back at your first annual review. The review has been done. If necessary, you've made a rebuttal. You've signed the form indicating that you had the review (your signature doesn't mean you agree with it, it just means you were awake while your boss droned on and on about your wonderful qualities).

If you've done your homework, you know what kind of salary increase to expect. In the worst of times, there may be a freeze on salary increases across the whole company because they aren't selling as many swag lamps as they used to. But let's assume that's not the case. Your boss will be given guidelines as to how much he can increase your salary. He has probably discussed it with his boss and gotten the approval to give you a certain percentage. In fact, when you were first hired, he may have calculated such an increase and put it in the budget.

Let's say he can give you anywhere from 0 percent to 5 percent. If he's held to that, no amount of discussion on your part will bump it up. Depending on the company and the type of job you have, he may have other means to reward you. There may be one-time cash bonuses he can give you for successfully completing major projects, or there may be salary increases he can give you at nonreview times for certain accomplishments, but in many cases, your one chance for an increase in salary is tied to the review. (Remember that the next time you roll over in bed and hit the snooze alarm one too many times.)

The percentage may well be tied to the numerical total on the review. If 1 is lowest and 5 is highest, and there are 20 categories, a perfect employee will have 100 points.

Aren't you glad you didn't sleep through math class?

Your company may have more rigid policies on salary increases: A total score of 90 to 100 will get 5 percent; 80 to 89 will get 4 percent and so forth. Or it may be more arbitrary than that. The point is: Know the rules, and how strictly they are enforced, before you enter the room for the review. Then, if your boss gives you 2 percent and you got a 90 on your evaluation, you've got some facts to back up your side of the discussion.

Same rules apply here: Keep calm, rational, polite, etc., while you push the reasons you should have more money.

If the increase is based on a vague "good" or "not so good" rating where numbers aren't assigned, you're on shakier ground. Maybe your company doesn't quantify it so much so the boss has more leeway in deciding how much you should get.

If he really likes you and tends to reward his employees more generously than others, it can mean you get, say, 10 percent; or, if he's a bit of a Scrooge, it can go the other way. Good companies realize bosses have subjective reasons for how they dole out the increases; that's why they tend to quantify how it's done so increases are the same, or almost the same, no matter whom you report to.

All in all, there's only so much you can do, short of walking out in a huff and trying to get a job somewhere else. You can protest to your boss, first of all, then seek counsel in human resources as to what to do next.

You are risking a lot if you put up a big fuss. Sure, it's hard to come to terms with a review or increase that wasn't what you were expecting when you think back on all the hard work you've done. If you make a federal case out of it, however, you may have effectively sealed your fate at the company and you simply need to start over somewhere else.

The better course of action may be to have a frank discussion (again, in a polite, civil, calm, etc., manner) with your boss about your concerns, *emphasizing how you can work together to improve your review the next time.* Ask him if there's a way you can demonstrate your improved performance so that you can have a letter of commendation placed in the file and an "extraordinary" salary increase (not one tied to a review). Usually, salary increases are better, overall, than bonuses because, like grudges, you carry the increase with you to your next job within the company.

And, the letter of commendation in the file means it's less likely a second review that's not top-notch will be done. You're also building a file for future bosses to read, too.

I'm getting less money because I'm a *what*?

There is a time to make a federal (or state) case. If you are convinced that you are being discriminated against because of your race, gender, religion, etc., then, yes, you must protest. I would suggest that you try to work it out within the company first; if you are not satisfied with the results, then you may need to file a complaint.

Often, such accusations are hard to prove. Sometimes, it's as "easy" as discovering that, out of five persons doing the same job, you, as the only woman, are making only 80 percent of what the guys are getting. If all things are otherwise equal (you were hired at the same time, you really do have the same duties and responsibilities), you've got a case.

Most employees in their first year on the job don't have enough experience to know if such discrimination is taking place. This will be more obvious as opportunities for promotions and other situations occur where you begin to suspect that, all other things being equal, you are continually shut out.

Sexual harassment is another matter. In extreme cases, a boss who has made advances that you spurned will give you a bad performance rating as retaliation. If you're wise, it won't even get to that point. The harassment should be dealt with immediately. Your company should have a written policy for you to follow. Again, if you don't get satisfaction, go to an outside source for help.

I hope for your sake that the lower-than-desired rating on a review, should you get one, is because you overslept too many times and not because you wouldn't sleep with someone—or because of irrelevant facts such as your skin color. But, as we all know, such incidents do take place in the workplace and we must be prepared for them.

On the other hand, let's toss a positive wrench into this argument. Suppose you got a rating that was great, one that you felt you deserved, and it was accompanied by the maximum increase?

Celebrate! And keep up the good work!

Chapter Ten

Getting Your Second Job

What? Already?

True. You may be perfectly content to continue working for some time in your current position. But there may come a time when you've discovered you've learned all there is to learn, and you'll be ready to move on. You may be ready to pursue a new position in a new company—possibly even in a new state! But don't overlook opportunities in your current company!

Unless you are escaping from a difficult and impossible situation where you are fighting—and losing—discrimination, working for a company that has gone Chapter 11 and will shortly be giving you the ax, or some other unanticipated and terrible thing, you may not want to jump ship (change companies) too quickly.

By now, you should have an idea of where you can go within your own company. You have at least 12 months of hard and smart work under your belt and you have impressed more than a few people here with your performance.

If you feel boxed in, check this out

Look at an organizational chart. What prospects do you have? Is your boss's job one that you can aspire to? Or is that unrealistic until you've been with the company for several more years? Are there positions within your department that pay more and have more responsibility that interest you? Do you know of any imminent departures?

Everyone's career is different. Some people advance in pretty much a straight line, moving from one position to another, every couple of years, on a regular basis. Other people jump from one department to another, sometimes taking leaps upwards, sometimes making lateral transfers ("lateral" means you trade one job for another that's on the same level, so you aren't earning more money or taking on any additional responsibilities).

As you consider making a move, whether a promotion or a lateral move, you should do some planning and research, much like you did when you began your first job search.

If your company has a tuition-reimbursement program, take advantage of it. Set your eyes on a career goal and take courses that will lead to that. If you really want to be in charge of a certain function at your company (or at a similar company), but you know you need so many semester hours of a certain subject, then you may as well get it now.

By doing this you are demonstrating that you are always interested in learning and adding to your knowledge and skills. That impresses people.

Also, talk with your boss about plans for the department. Let her know that, while you are satisfied with your job, you are interested in discussing what lies ahead for you personally and for the department. She had hinted at the creation of a new position, for example. You are interested in applying for it if and when it does occur. Or, you recommend that she create a second senior sales position because of an increase in business, a position you'd like to apply for.

I don't want your job, but I'll take your salary

This discussion (or series of discussions) will let her know that you are thinking ahead. It will give her some food for thought. ("Hmmm," she thinks after you leave, "a second senior sales position? Could work, could work.") It shows that, while you are happy at what you are doing (which should be obvious without you having to tell her), you are planning your future in a way that can enhance the department and not threaten her.

Keep an eye on job openings as posted by the human resources department. Even if you are not actively interested in applying for any of them, this will give you a good idea of what jobs come up from time to time, how much they pay (if the company lists them as A-12, A-13, etc., you will know the salary ranges), how other departments are structured, and so forth.

If you do apply for a job in another department, you will be required to let your current boss know this when you apply. It could also have the benefit of making her panic, deciding that she doesn't want to lose you. She might even, if allowed, give you more money or other incentives to stay where you are.

Upgrading your current position

Your boss might be able to upgrade your current position, changing it from an A-12 to an A-13. She will have to justify that, on paper, with lots of data. It's not likely to be a rush process and she can't guarantee that it will happen, even if she's a vice president. It will have to be reviewed by a hard-nosed committee in human resources composed of people from different departments around the company.

They will be concerned that upgrading your job means they'll have to upgrade 20 other jobs and it doesn't take a mathematician to figure out that that could cost the company a lot of money in salary and benefit increases.

Proof of the increased responsibilities since the job was created will be required, and you may spend considerable time helping your boss gather this information. If it does come about, you will probably retain the same job title, but the rating (A-13) will increase and the salary will increase. It can certainly be worth the effort!

I really, really like you, but I like her better

It's important for you to tell your boss, if you do look elsewhere, that you aren't dissatisfied with what you're doing, but that you are applying for a job that pays more money or one with increased responsibilities or even one that more closely matches your education and experience. It could be that you are applying for a job that matches what you plan to study (maybe you're going to get a master's degree in marketing and the other job will be more directly related to that field of study than your present job).

Before you take the plunge, go back over the first few chapters in this book. Much of the groundwork for a new job will be the same as for your first job. You will want to do a certain amount of research, resume rewriting, preparation for interviews, and so on, to present yourself in the best possible light for the next job.

You may even end up doing more than one version of your resume, depending on which jobs you are applying for.

Getting fired: The ultimate downer

What if you are called into your boss's office and she says, "You're fired." It's really, really not the end of the world, although it may seem close. Here you spent all that time in school and spent all that time on the job to find out that you are being told to get out of the building.

You can't help feeling bad, ashamed, guilty, angry and close to or in tears. No one expects you to shrug your shoulders, shake hands all around and leave without a care in the world.

It would be an unusual—but not unheard of—situation if you really didn't expect the firing to take place. There are different kinds of firing, of course. There's a reduction in force (RIF) where whole departments or a certain percentage of the company are let go. The company is in trouble, perhaps, or anticipating avoiding future trouble by cutting back on one of its biggest expenses—payroll. You, with about a year's experience at the company, may be one of the first in line to go. On the other hand, the company may seek to eliminate people who make a lot more money and, thus, your boss and his boss may be getting the ax. In any case, it can be pretty scary.

Actually, Jack, it's because I just don't like your face

Suppose it's personal. By that, I mean, it's not a wholesale RIF or a reorganization (where your department is deemed "unnecessary" and all of you are bid farewell), but a one-person RIF.

Again, there may be different reasons. Your boss may have been given orders to save a certain amount of money by reducing her staff and she managed to save everyone else's job but yours.

Or it could be what we all fear—we didn't perform as we should have and we are outright fired. That's the one that really hurts.

If you are convinced you have been fired because of your rebuff of sexual advances or because of the other discriminatory reasons noted in the last chapter (race, gender, etc.), then you must decide if you'll fight it on those grounds. For your sake, and for the sake of others who may be discriminated against by the same individual or company, I hope you will fight it.

And then there was the week you forgot to come to work

If it is because of performance, the company will have to have grounds for the action. They, too, know about building paper trails. If you are required to make a certain number of sales a week, and you know that, and you have been given a certain number of warnings because you aren't making your quotas, then it's fairly cut-and-dried that you'll be let go. You should be less surprised than anyone.

If you work in an area that isn't so easily quantified, however, it is both more difficult for your employer to "prove" your poor performance and for you to "prove" your good one. Both of you will seek to document how well (or how poorly) you are doing.

In so many cases, the person who is fired, if he is going to be really honest with himself, isn't too surprised. He has received verbal and then written warnings about his performance, and he has been given an ultimatum. ("If this does not improve by March 1, we will have no other recourse but to terminate your employment with The Cueto Companies.")

If you truly are surprised, you have every right to demand reasons for the firing, in writing. If you have positive reviews and other written materials that demonstrate that you performed the job satisfactorily, then you have to decide if you will fight the firing.

If, of course, you have committed illegal acts, you don't have any recourse and, in fact, you'll be glad that a firing is all that is taking place. If you fudged your sales records or your expense accounts, no one is going to want to keep you on staff. I'm talking here, instead, about those gray-area "performance" issues.

Now I can see "Oprah" every day of the week

Let's say that you were expecting the firing. For whatever reason, you did not perform as you should have and you are almost—not quite, but almost—relieved to be relieved of your duties. Maybe you really, really hated the job, but hadn't gotten around to getting another one. Now's your chance!

What next? I keep saying this, but I'll say it again: Keep calm. Don't take your company letters of commendation and toss them all over the corporation's front lawn while letting all passersby know what you think.

Listen. Learn. Leave.

Your boss is likely to be very embarrassed and uncomfortable. Although she will recover (she's still employed, for one thing), she probably doesn't relish this assignment, even if she's been considering getting rid of you for months.

Go through the exit interviews with her and then with human resources. Ask lots of questions. Find out how you could have done better.

That's easy for you to say, buster

It may seem rather glib to say, "Make this a learning experience." But do make it a learning experience. How can you turn this around to help you the next time? Listen closely to what they are saying. Did you ignore outright signals to do better? Did you go into denial that anything was wrong?

It's probably the ultimate ego-deflating experience (other than showing up at your wedding, and having your intended pull you aside and say, "Say, hon, I've been thinking..."). But you will survive. You will go on to other jobs where you will not be fired. And you will have learned a great deal from your working at the company and from leaving. Trust me.

But let's leave this on a positive note. After all, *if you were smart enough to buy this book, you're smart enough not to get fired.* And you're smart enough to follow the advice I've given you here.

Dear Sir, I have worked here for 60 days and I need a change

If you are thinking of applying for a job outside the company, don't be in too big a hurry unless, of course, you are in a hopelessly bad situation.

Traditionally, resumes that show a lot of jobs that lasted about 12 months (or less) tend to make prospective employers nervous. "If we were to hire you," they might ask, "how long would you plan to stay?" They may fear that your lack of tenure at any one location indicates that you easily lose interest or you are a difficult employee.

If you just have a short attention span and you keep wanting new challenges, try to confine your moving about to one company, at least for a few years at a time. If you put in five-year stints, for example, at companies and you have two or three job titles within each one, that appears a lot more positive than if you work for three companies within each five-year period.

Currently, however, employers are frequently a little more sympathetic to job changes, especially when you indicate good reasons for them. Your spouse may be on a fast track, he or she keeps getting promoted and transferred and you have agreed to move along. You may have been the victim of a corporate down-sizing or company lay-off, an occurrence that employers are all too aware of these days.

While it is definitely in your favor to show job stability to a prospective employer, there are circumstances where it makes sense for you to leave a job for another, better opportunity. For example, while you yearned to land a position as a writer for a travel magazine, the closest offer you received was to write promotional copy for a company that distributes luggage. While you've enjoyed your work and have indeed done a wonderful job in your first year as a member of the work force, an opening comes up at the travel magazine you've been dreaming about working for.

Should you pass up the opportunity because you need to show stability on your resume? Because you owe it to your boss? While loyalty and stability are admirable traits, your first loyalty is to yourself in pursuing your own goals.

Go for the job. Present yourself as a goal-oriented and directed individual who is enthusiastic about your chosen field, and you'll more than likely overcome any concerns your prospective employer may have about your stability.

Chapter Eleven

Conclusion

Let me leave you with just one more bit of advice and then I'll let you get to the library to start your research: A good career is a joy to have. Don't approach your first job, or any job, with the idea that you're only working because you have to, and all you can think about is retiring or doing what you really want to do after hours or on the weekends.

There is great personal satisfaction from doing a job well and building a career. Enjoy your work. Take pride in it. Look upon your job as an important, interesting part of your life, not as a barely tolerable interruption.

The job market is tough now. No doubt, it's toughest for those of you entering it for the first time. And it's going to require hard work, smart work and some patience.

Yes, it's tough to find a job these days. But not impossible. Armed with the job-search ammunition provided in this book, and your determination to find fulfilling and satisfying work, and to learn from every job experience, there's no doubt in my mind that you find what you're looking for—your *first* job, and many more after that.

Index

Your First Job

UNION COUNTY COLLEGE